T0381557

My Inspirations for You

366 Daily Inspirational Quotes -
One for each day of the year

Valerie Rhee Driver

BALBOA.PRESS
A DIVISION OF HAY HOUSE

Balboa Press books may be ordered through booksellers or by contacting:

Balboa Press
A Division of Hay House
1663 Liberty Drive
Bloomington, IN 47403
www.balboapress.com.au
AU TFN: 1 800 844 925 (Toll Free inside Australia)
AU Local: 0283 107 086 (+61 2 8310 7086 from outside Australia)

Print information available on the last page.

ISBN: 978-1-5043-2171-6 (sc)
ISBN: 978-1-5043-2170-9 (e)

Balboa Press rev. date: 07/8/2020

Introduction to Inspiration

This book is written with the intention of inspiring.

- Inspiring positive thoughts and feelings.
- Inspiring a change in thinking.
- Inspiring a smile.
- Inspiring hope.

There are several ways you can use this book.

You can read a quote daily, to inspire you or you can open this book if you feel you are in need of a little inspiration, or even a lot of inspiration.

You can start at the first one and go through the book chronologically, or you can open the book at random and read the quote on the page you open to.

If you are feeling low or sad, or maybe overwhelmed, or struggling with a problem then reach for this book and read a quote. If you choose to let it fall open to a page, whichever page it opens to is the ideal page for you to read at that point in time.

Starting each day with something that inspires you is a great way to start your day. As is having someone or something to turn to when you are feeling down. Being happy and positive all day every day isn't realistic. We are all human after all. However, when you are feeling low, reading something positive and inspiring can help to lift you up.

So whichever way you choose to use this book may it inspire you to think positively and to believe in yourself, all that is possible, and all that you are capable of.

How to Read/Use: This Book/These Daily Inspirations

There are many options for how to get the most out of this book.
Below are just some of them (In no specific order).

Possibility 1:
You can simply read an inspiration each morning to get your day off to a good start.

Possibility 2:
You can choose to read an inspiration at any time of day.

Possibility 3:
You can read all the inspirational quotes in a whole section in one sitting – once a month, or once a week, or whenever you feel motivated to do so.

Possibility 4:
You can combine reading this book with reading other inspirational materials like oracle cards and self-help books, or can read it on its own.

Possibility 5:
You can read the inspirational quote and complete the task at the same time, or at different times.

Possibility 6:
You can make reading this book part of your daily practice. Reading an inspirational quote and completing the associated task at the same time, or you can approach it more randomly.

Possibility 7:
You can leave the book open to the page and refer to it often throughout the day, or you can read an inspiration once a day and ponder it.

Possibility 8:
You can read the inspiration in the morning, ponder it at times throughout the day and then complete the task in the evening.

Possibility 9:
You can focus on one inspiration a day, or for a week, or even longer if you wish.

What other possibilities can you think of?

As well as possibilities for when and where you can approach reading this book there are numerous options for how to approach reading it.

Option 1:
You can start at the first inspiration on page 3 and proceed to the next page reading an inspiration each day.

Option 2:
You can start at any inspiration on any page and continue reading one page per day.

Option 3:
You can open the book at a random page each day and read and ponder that inspirational quote.

Option 4:
You can open the book to a random page at random times.
Times when you are:

- Seeking some inspiration; or
- Seeking some clarity; or
- Looking for an answer; or
- Feeling stuck: or Feeling lost; or Feeling sad; or Feeling lonely; or Feeling empty. Or any other feeling.

Option 5:
You can just open the book at a random page at any random time regardless of how you are feeling or what you may be looking for.

Option 6:
You can choose a section that's relevant to your present state of mind, or the state of mind you are seeking, and read the whole section – or just part of that section.

Option 7:
You can choose how you wish to read this book.

Whichever way you choose to approach the reading of this book I sincerely hope that it is beneficial for you, and it inspires you to get the best out of every day and to be the best version of you possible.

What you can expect when reading this book

How you approach reading this book will influence what you can expect, as obviously depending on your approach and your expectations, the outcomes will vary.

Whichever way you approach reading this book you can anticipate that you may feel inspired; you may gain some clarity; you may find an answer to a question you have; or you may just feel some pleasure and enjoy the experience.

If you approach reading this book with an open mind and expectancy of what you could gain, then it is highly likely you will enjoy your experience and gain a great deal.

After each inspirational quote there is a task relevant to that quote for you to complete. The tasks are designed to assist you to ponder the significance of the quote for you and your current life situation. I would like to suggest that each time you read a specific inspiration you attempt to complete the task, as your situation will be different each time. What was relevant previously will not necessarily be relevant the next time you read that same quote. As we learn and grow our perspective changes and thus how we view and interpret things also changes.

When completing the tasks you can take as long as you like or complete them as quickly as you like. Obviously if you take longer to complete any task you stand to gain more from the experience. If we skim over something without giving it much thought then surface understanding is most likely what we will gain; yet if we take longer and choose to consider it more deeply then you will most likely gain a deeper understanding of that quotes relevance for you.

When you complete the tasks for each inspiration you will quite obviously gain more than if you just read the quote. Yet there will be times when you only have time to read the quote, and at those times you will still gain something from the experience. Whether reading the quote only or reading the quote and completing the task please take the time to centre yourself first – especially if you are opening the book at a random page. You may wish to think of a situation or a question before opening the book. Before completing any task please take the time to be still and to centre yourself before beginning.

As I said previously how you choose to approach reading this book will greatly influence what you get out of it. Whichever approach you choose I hope that your experience is the positive and uplifting opportunity I envision it being. Thank you for reading my book and sharing its wisdom with others.

Love Rhee

12 months of a Year – 12 Chapters to choose from...

Yes, one chapter for each month of the year if you choose.

1. Courage over Fear

2. Action over Perfection

3. Trust over Doubt

4. Clarity over Confusion

5. Joy over Sadness

6. Hope over Despair

7. Focus over Distraction

8. Less over More

9. Gratitude over Regret

10. Persistence over Failure

11. Self-confidence over self-sabotage

12. Celebration over Criticism

366 Inspirational Quotes for you to read...

And be inspired by – if you choose.

366 Tasks to help you ponder the Quote...

If you Choose!

1. Choose Courage Over Fear

	QUOTE	JOURNAL PROMPT/TASK
1	F false E evidence A appearing R real I can't take the credit for this acronym but it says it all!	*Do this now:* Write down a big audacious goal (BAG). Now write down all the possible things that could stop you from achieving it – all the 'BUGS' Ponder these bugs. Are they real problems? Or are they imagined problems? What are your problems based on? – Fact or Fiction? What is the underlying theme of your 'problems'? Is it fear! False Evidence Appearing Real? Now – Look at you BAG again and write down all the reasons you can achieve it and the steps you will take to do just that! Achieve it! Put it in the **bag**!

	QUOTE	JOURNAL PROMPT/TASK
2	C consistency O options U undertaking R repetition A assertiveness G gaul E enthusiasm Love & light Valerie 🖤	*Think this now:* What is courage? What does courage mean to you? The Oxford Dictionary defines Courage as: the ability to do something that frightens one; bravery. strength in the face of pain or grief. Is your courage bigger than your fear? Or do you allow your fears to over-ride your courage? Now – Write your own definition of courage. Then reread it regularly. And be Courageous!

	QUOTE	JOURNAL PROMPT/TASK
3	Trust in your abilities and skills. Stand up and put yourself forward for all opportunities that resonate with you. Break out of the same old, same old. Do something different! Love & light Valerie ♥	*Do this now:* Write a list of your abilities and skills. Just write everything that comes into your head (you can refine the list later). Don't discard any thoughts. Just write them down. Once you finish writing reread your list. Which abilities and skills do you resonate most with? Which ones do you feel most passionate about? Which ones inspire you? Which ones can you act on? Which ones break you out of your same old patterns? Now – Go forth and do something different and honour your gifts and talents at the same time.

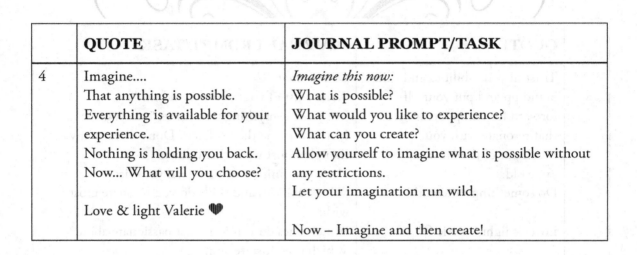

	QUOTE	JOURNAL PROMPT/TASK
4	Imagine.... That anything is possible. Everything is available for your experience. Nothing is holding you back. Now... What will you choose? Love & light Valerie 🖤	*Imagine this now:* What is possible? What would you like to experience? What can you create? Allow yourself to imagine what is possible without any restrictions. Let your imagination run wild. Now – Imagine and then create!

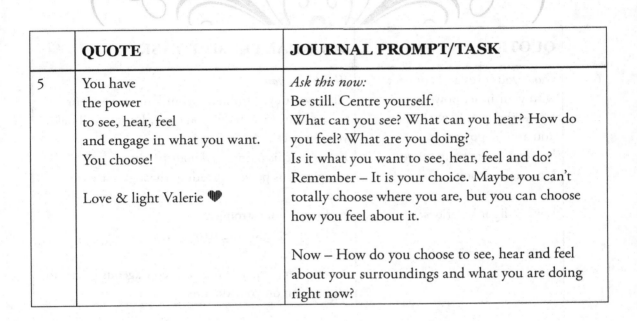

	QUOTE	JOURNAL PROMPT/TASK
5	You have the power to see, hear, feel and engage in what you want. You choose! Love & light Valerie ♥	*Ask this now:* Be still. Centre yourself. What can you see? What can you hear? How do you feel? What are you doing? Is it what you want to see, hear, feel and do? Remember – It is your choice. Maybe you can't totally choose where you are, but you can choose how you feel about it. Now – How do you choose to see, hear and feel about your surroundings and what you are doing right now?

	QUOTE	JOURNAL PROMPT/TASK
6	Close your eyes and connect with your inner power. Know that you have the power, You are the power. You can create your desires. Now, take action. Love & light Valerie ♥	*Think this now:* Close your eyes and place your hands over your solar plexus (just above your belly button and below your breast). Focus on this point. Feel your power. Imagine this power spreading throughout your body. Feel it growing stronger. Feel yourself growing stronger. Now – Go forth and use your courageous power to take action on your dreams.

	QUOTE	JOURNAL PROMPT/TASK
7	Resolve to take empowered action to support yourself. Love & light Valerie 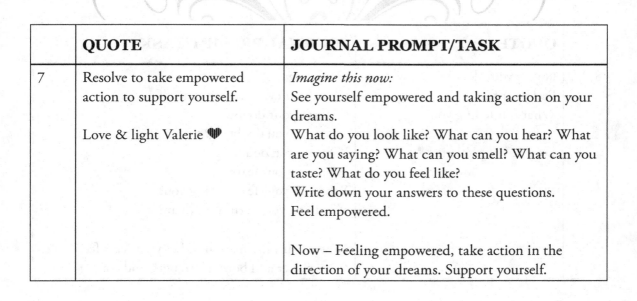	*Imagine this now:* See yourself empowered and taking action on your dreams. What do you look like? What can you hear? What are you saying? What can you smell? What can you taste? What do you feel like? Write down your answers to these questions. Feel empowered. Now – Feeling empowered, take action in the direction of your dreams. Support yourself.

	QUOTE	JOURNAL PROMPT/TASK
8	Notice your doubt. Feel your fear. What is it telling you? Love & light Valerie 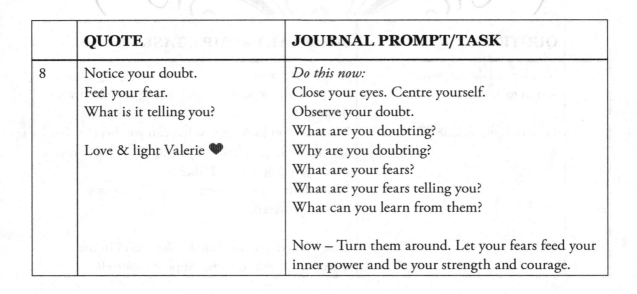	*Do this now:* Close your eyes. Centre yourself. Observe your doubt. What are you doubting? Why are you doubting? What are your fears? What are your fears telling you? What can you learn from them? Now – Turn them around. Let your fears feed your inner power and be your strength and courage.

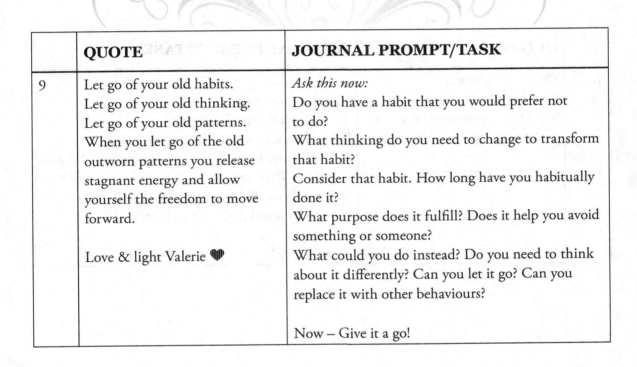

	QUOTE	JOURNAL PROMPT/TASK
9	Let go of your old habits. Let go of your old thinking. Let go of your old patterns. When you let go of the old outworn patterns you release stagnant energy and allow yourself the freedom to move forward. Love & light Valerie ♥	*Ask this now:* Do you have a habit that you would prefer not to do? What thinking do you need to change to transform that habit? Consider that habit. How long have you habitually done it? What purpose does it fulfill? Does it help you avoid something or someone? What could you do instead? Do you need to think about it differently? Can you let it go? Can you replace it with other behaviours? Now – Give it a go!

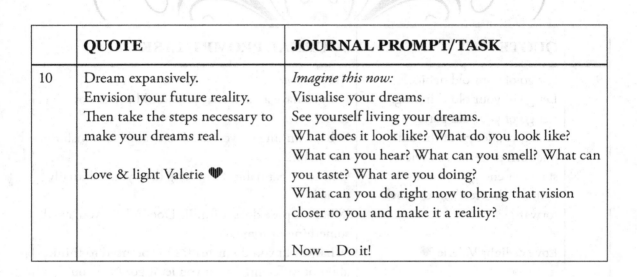

	QUOTE	JOURNAL PROMPT/TASK
10	Dream expansively. Envision your future reality. Then take the steps necessary to make your dreams real. Love & light Valerie ♥	*Imagine this now:* Visualise your dreams. See yourself living your dreams. What does it look like? What do you look like? What can you hear? What can you smell? What can you taste? What are you doing? What can you do right now to bring that vision closer to you and make it a reality? Now – Do it!

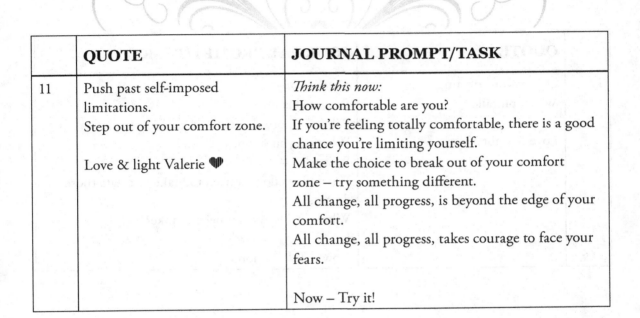

	QUOTE	JOURNAL PROMPT/TASK
11	Push past self-imposed limitations. Step out of your comfort zone. Love & light Valerie ♥	*Think this now:* How comfortable are you? If you're feeling totally comfortable, there is a good chance you're limiting yourself. Make the choice to break out of your comfort zone – try something different. All change, all progress, is beyond the edge of your comfort. All change, all progress, takes courage to face your fears. Now – Try it!

	QUOTE	JOURNAL PROMPT/TASK
12	Dream your dreams. Walk you talk. Love & light Valerie 🖤	*Do this now:* Ponder this – What are your dreams? What do you desire to create? Write this – What plans do you need to make to create those dreams? What actions do you need to take? Now – Take action.

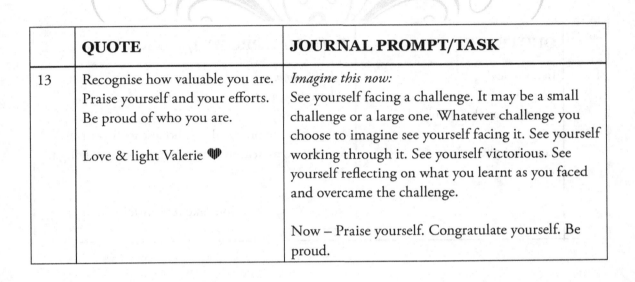

	QUOTE	JOURNAL PROMPT/TASK
13	Recognise how valuable you are. Praise yourself and your efforts. Be proud of who you are. Love & light Valerie ♥	*Imagine this now:* See yourself facing a challenge. It may be a small challenge or a large one. Whatever challenge you choose to imagine see yourself facing it. See yourself working through it. See yourself victorious. See yourself reflecting on what you learnt as you faced and overcame the challenge. Now – Praise yourself. Congratulate yourself. Be proud.

	QUOTE	JOURNAL PROMPT/TASK
14	Be practical. Be real. Take personal responsibility. Love & light Valerie 🖤	*Ask this now:* Where in your life do you need to take responsibility? Are you being practical and honest with yourself? Are you being real with yourself, or are you lying to yourself? Now – Where can you take responsibility right now?

	QUOTE	JOURNAL PROMPT/TASK
15	You hold the key to your change. Love & light Valerie 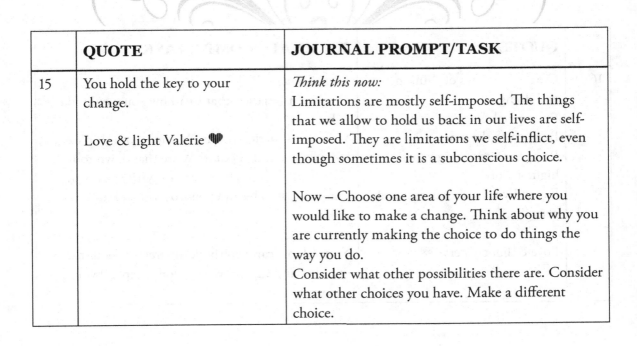	*Think this now:* Limitations are mostly self-imposed. The things that we allow to hold us back in our lives are self-imposed. They are limitations we self-inflict, even though sometimes it is a subconscious choice. Now – Choose one area of your life where you would like to make a change. Think about why you are currently making the choice to do things the way you do. Consider what other possibilities there are. Consider what other choices you have. Make a different choice.

	QUOTE	JOURNAL PROMPT/TASK
16	Create new ways of thinking and doing. Be original. Be open to the new. Be open to receiving your highest worth. Expand your vision of you and your life. Love & light Valerie ♥	*Do this now:* Think of a situation that isn't how you would like it to be. Write the situation down. What are you thinking? How do you feel about it? Write that down too. Next to what you have written – Write how you would like it to be and how you would like to feel about it. Now – How can you think differently about the situation and expand your vision – expand your opportunities?

	QUOTE	JOURNAL PROMPT/TASK
17	Be self-responsible. See your greatness within. Love & light Valerie 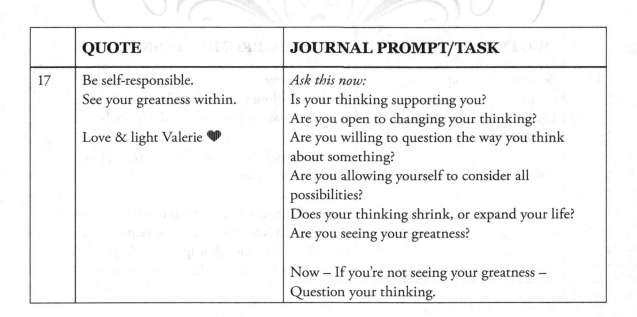	*Ask this now:* Is your thinking supporting you? Are you open to changing your thinking? Are you willing to question the way you think about something? Are you allowing yourself to consider all possibilities? Does your thinking shrink, or expand your life? Are you seeing your greatness? Now – If you're not seeing your greatness – Question your thinking.

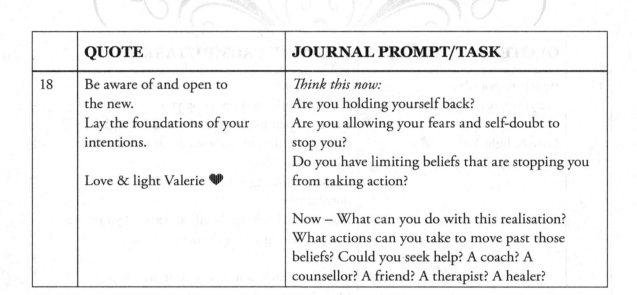

	QUOTE	JOURNAL PROMPT/TASK
18	Be aware of and open to the new. Lay the foundations of your intentions. Love & light Valerie ♥	*Think this now:* Are you holding yourself back? Are you allowing your fears and self-doubt to stop you? Do you have limiting beliefs that are stopping you from taking action? Now – What can you do with this realisation? What actions can you take to move past those beliefs? Could you seek help? A coach? A counsellor? A friend? A therapist? A healer?

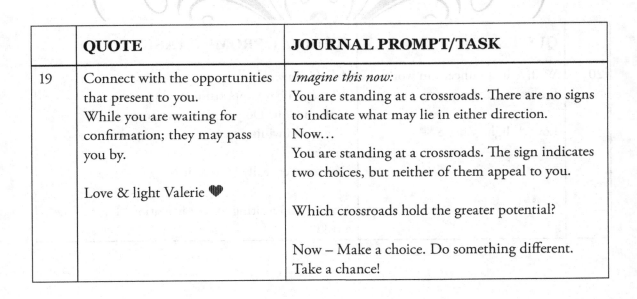

	QUOTE	JOURNAL PROMPT/TASK
19	Connect with the opportunities that present to you. While you are waiting for confirmation; they may pass you by. Love & light Valerie ♥	*Imagine this now:* You are standing at a crossroads. There are no signs to indicate what may lie in either direction. Now… You are standing at a crossroads. The sign indicates two choices, but neither of them appeal to you. Which crossroads hold the greater potential? Now – Make a choice. Do something different. Take a chance!

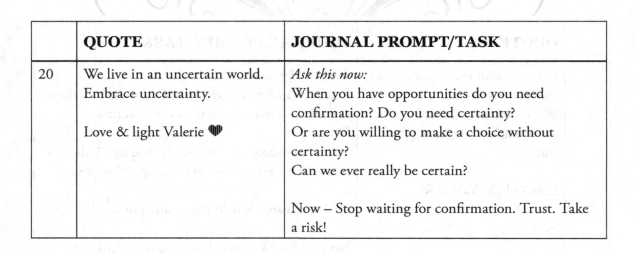

	QUOTE	JOURNAL PROMPT/TASK
20	We live in an uncertain world. Embrace uncertainty. Love & light Valerie 🖤	*Ask this now:* When you have opportunities do you need confirmation? Do you need certainty? Or are you willing to make a choice without certainty? Can we ever really be certain? Now – Stop waiting for confirmation. Trust. Take a risk!

	QUOTE	JOURNAL PROMPT/TASK
21	As you encounter any daily challenges - Face them. Work through them. Grow and learn from them. Love & light Valerie 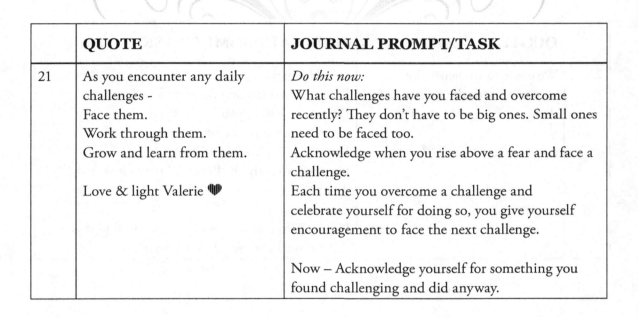	*Do this now:* What challenges have you faced and overcome recently? They don't have to be big ones. Small ones need to be faced too. Acknowledge when you rise above a fear and face a challenge. Each time you overcome a challenge and celebrate yourself for doing so, you give yourself encouragement to face the next challenge. Now – Acknowledge yourself for something you found challenging and did anyway.

	QUOTE	JOURNAL PROMPT/TASK
22	We come to wholeness by accepting both the light and the dark. Love & light Valerie 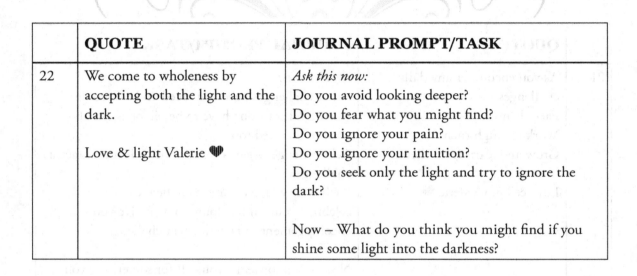	*Ask this now:* Do you avoid looking deeper? Do you fear what you might find? Do you ignore your pain? Do you ignore your intuition? Do you seek only the light and try to ignore the dark? Now – What do you think you might find if you shine some light into the darkness?

	QUOTE	JOURNAL PROMPT/TASK
23	Honour your path and your personal experiences. Let them go with love. Love & light Valerie 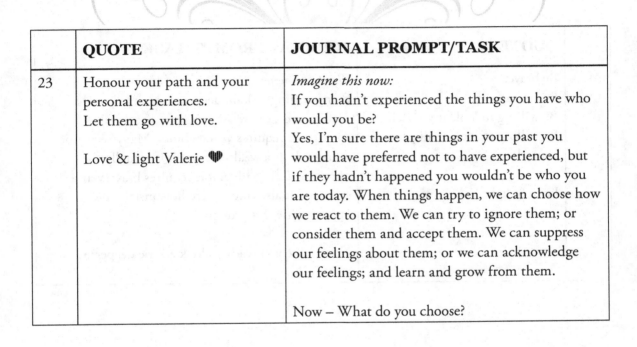	*Imagine this now:* If you hadn't experienced the things you have who would you be? Yes, I'm sure there are things in your past you would have preferred not to have experienced, but if they hadn't happened you wouldn't be who you are today. When things happen, we can choose how we react to them. We can try to ignore them; or consider them and accept them. We can suppress our feelings about them; or we can acknowledge our feelings; and learn and grow from them. Now – What do you choose?

	QUOTE	JOURNAL PROMPT/TASK
24	Be brave. Be courageous. Be willing to look at yourself. Be willing to look at all parts of yourself. Love & light Valerie 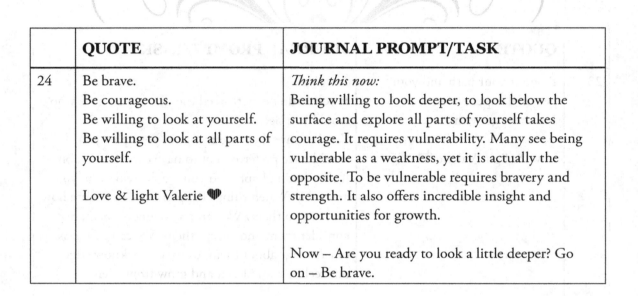	*Think this now:* Being willing to look deeper, to look below the surface and explore all parts of yourself takes courage. It requires vulnerability. Many see being vulnerable as a weakness, yet it is actually the opposite. To be vulnerable requires bravery and strength. It also offers incredible insight and opportunities for growth. Now – Are you ready to look a little deeper? Go on – Be brave.

	QUOTE	JOURNAL PROMPT/TASK
25	Never give away your power. Always know that you are your power. Love & light Valerie 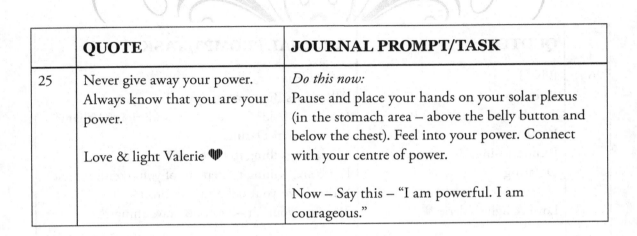	*Do this now:* Pause and place your hands on your solar plexus (in the stomach area – above the belly button and below the chest). Feel into your power. Connect with your centre of power. Now – Say this – "I am powerful. I am courageous."

	QUOTE	JOURNAL PROMPT/TASK
26	B bold R resourceful A audacious V valiant E enterprising D daring Love & light Valerie 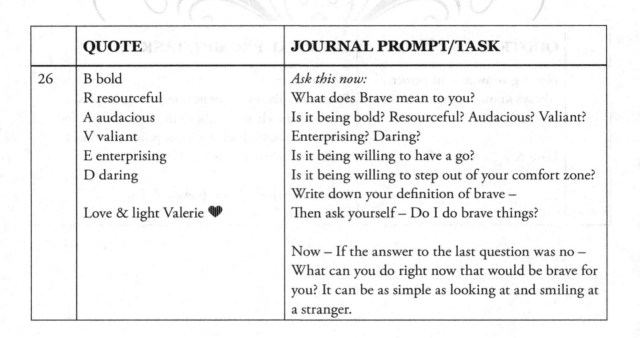	*Ask this now:* What does Brave mean to you? Is it being bold? Resourceful? Audacious? Valiant? Enterprising? Daring? Is it being willing to have a go? Is it being willing to step out of your comfort zone? Write down your definition of brave – Then ask yourself – Do I do brave things? Now – If the answer to the last question was no – What can you do right now that would be brave for you? It can be as simple as looking at and smiling at a stranger.

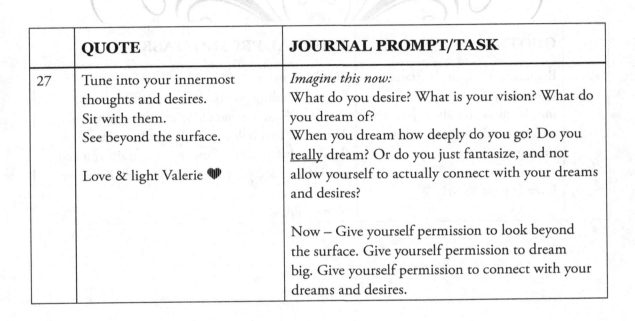

	QUOTE	JOURNAL PROMPT/TASK
27	Tune into your innermost thoughts and desires. Sit with them. See beyond the surface. Love & light Valerie ♥	*Imagine this now:* What do you desire? What is your vision? What do you dream of? When you dream how deeply do you go? Do you <u>really</u> dream? Or do you just fantasize, and not allow yourself to actually connect with your dreams and desires? Now – Give yourself permission to look beyond the surface. Give yourself permission to dream big. Give yourself permission to connect with your dreams and desires.

	QUOTE	JOURNAL PROMPT/TASK
28	Break free from the restraints. Consider your success as imminent as you allow your true and authentic nature to shine through. Love & light Valerie 🖤	*Think this now:* What is holding you back from realising your dreams? What are you allowing to restrain you? Almost all that holds us back is self-imposed. Ponder what you are allowing to restrain you and break free. Face your fears. See yourself being free. Now – Shine!

	QUOTE	JOURNAL PROMPT/TASK
29	Grow through what you go through. Love & light Valerie ♥	*Imagine this now:* Imagine if there was no meaning to anything you had experienced and life was just a series of events. Things for you to 'go through'. Yet some events bring us joy and others bring us sorrow; some are fun some are torturous; some are easy and some are frustrating. All events can evoke feelings within us. How we choose to process and respond to each and every event determines whether we grow or not. Now – Are you willing to grow, or are you just going to 'go through' each event?

	QUOTE	JOURNAL PROMPT/TASK
30	Be stronger than your excuses. Love & light Valerie 🖤	*Ask this now:* What excuses do you make? I'm too tired. I've tried before and it didn't work. He/ She/ They might get upset if I do that. I have to do this first. (like the dishes, or the washing.) I have a headache. It is too far to drive/walk. It's too hard. Often the energy we put into making excuses could be used to accomplish the thing we are making excuses about. Now – What are you avoiding when you make an excuse? What could you achieve if you didn't make the excuse and just did 'it'?

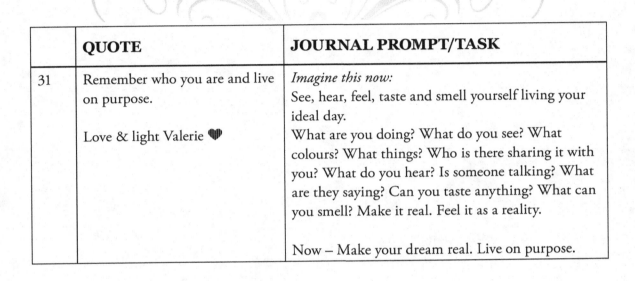

	QUOTE	JOURNAL PROMPT/TASK
31	Remember who you are and live on purpose. Love & light Valerie ♥	*Imagine this now:* See, hear, feel, taste and smell yourself living your ideal day. What are you doing? What do you see? What colours? What things? Who is there sharing it with you? What do you hear? Is someone talking? What are they saying? Can you taste anything? What can you smell? Make it real. Feel it as a reality. Now – Make your dream real. Live on purpose.

2. Choose Action Over Perfection

	QUOTE	JOURNAL PROMPT/TASK
1	P precise E exceptional R response F failure E exact C cope T total I intent O only way N not possible Love & light Valerie 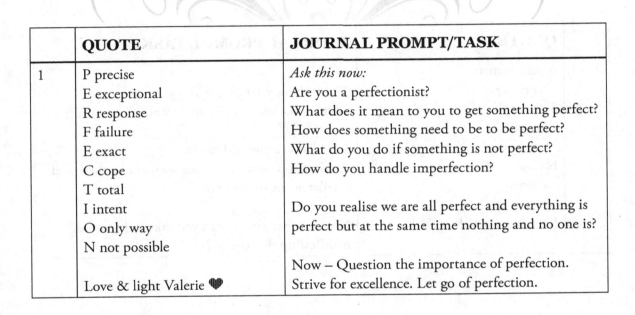	*Ask this now:* Are you a perfectionist? What does it mean to you to get something perfect? How does something need to be to be perfect? What do you do if something is not perfect? How do you handle imperfection? Do you realise we are all perfect and everything is perfect but at the same time nothing and no one is? Now – Question the importance of perfection. Strive for excellence. Let go of perfection.

	QUOTE	JOURNAL PROMPT/TASK
2	A achievement C conquer T triumph I initiate O options N now S success Love & light Valerie 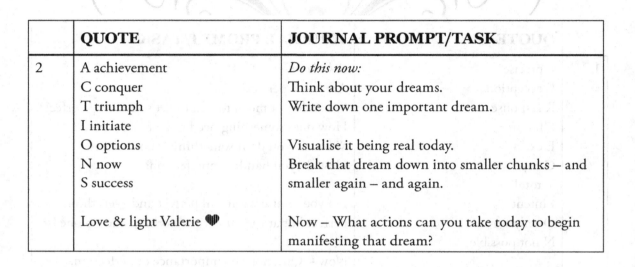	*Do this now:* Think about your dreams. Write down one important dream. Visualise it being real today. Break that dream down into smaller chunks – and smaller again – and again. Now – What actions can you take today to begin manifesting that dream?

	QUOTE	JOURNAL PROMPT/TASK
3	Thinking about the past can result in you feeling regretful or guilty. Thinking about the future can result in you worrying and feeling anxious. Very good reasons to think about the present – Where you are right now? Love & light Valerie 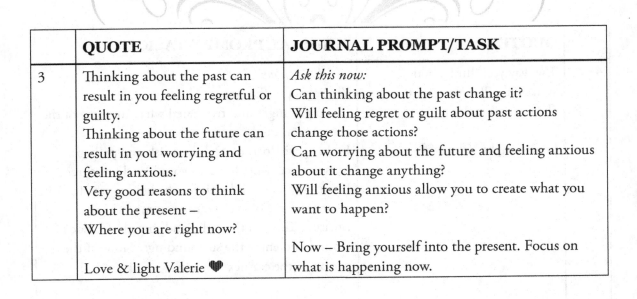	*Ask this now:* Can thinking about the past change it? Will feeling regret or guilt about past actions change those actions? Can worrying about the future and feeling anxious about it change anything? Will feeling anxious allow you to create what you want to happen? Now – Bring yourself into the present. Focus on what is happening now.

	QUOTE	JOURNAL PROMPT/TASK
4	The way you think about a situation will determine the choices you make. Love & light Valerie ♥	*Think this now:* You're in a traffic jam. If you get angry and frustrated what are some of the choices you might make? Feel angry? Road rage? Take a risk and perhaps cause an accident? Increase your blood pressure? If you stay calm and wait for the hold up to clear what are some of the choices you might make? Breathe? Turn on the radio and sing along? Look around and enjoy the surroundings? Smile at the person in the car next to you? Now – Choose a situation in your life – How will you think about it? What choices will you make?

	QUOTE	JOURNAL PROMPT/TASK
5	Honour yourself and your dreams. Take actions that support your dreams. Love & light Valerie ♥	*Do this now:* Choose an important dream. Think about it. What steps have you taken to bring that dream to life? Do you connect with that dream daily? Is it on your vision board? Do you have a vision board? Have you written it down? Where have you written it down? Is it somewhere where you see it daily? Have you broken it down into doable chunks? Or Is it just a dream? Now – Are you living your dreams or just dreaming your dreams? What can you do to manifest your dream?

	QUOTE	JOURNAL PROMPT/TASK
6	Remember – Too much focus on the future can lead to anxiety. Too much focus on the future can lead to inaction. Love & light Valerie ♥	*Imagine this now:* You're in the future. Maybe a few months or a year or two. You spent months/years worrying about this moment and feeling anxious. You played out all the possibilities of what could go wrong over and over in your head. You dramatized all the problems in your head. You thought the worst. Did that help? Did it stop anything from happening? Now – If worry helped us achieve our goals then most of us would be living our dreams right now. Are we? Are you?

	QUOTE	JOURNAL PROMPT/TASK
7	You know what to do. Trust in your next moves. Love & light Valerie 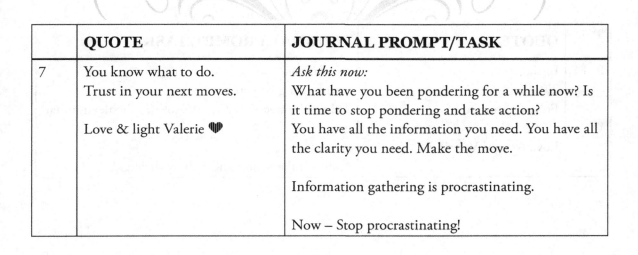	*Ask this now:* What have you been pondering for a while now? Is it time to stop pondering and take action? You have all the information you need. You have all the clarity you need. Make the move. Information gathering is procrastinating. Now – Stop procrastinating!

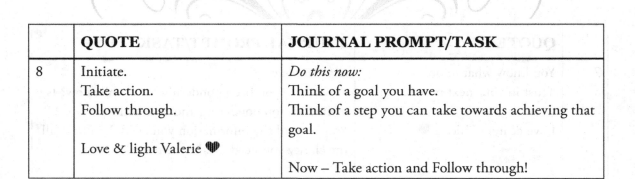

	QUOTE	JOURNAL PROMPT/TASK
8	Initiate. Take action. Follow through. Love & light Valerie 🖤	*Do this now:* Think of a goal you have. Think of a step you can take towards achieving that goal. Now – Take action and Follow through!

	QUOTE	JOURNAL PROMPT/TASK
9	You are in charge of your reality. You decide how you will proceed. Love & light Valerie ♥	*Think this now:* When you choose your thoughts and actions and how you will proceed you put yourself in charge of your reality and your life? Now – Proceed

	QUOTE	JOURNAL PROMPT/TASK
10	Remember: For every action in your life there is a reaction. For every thought you have there is a consequence. Ensure your future consequences are ones you're proud of. Love & light Valerie ♥	*Ask this now:* What will you choose today? Do you choose to be happy? Do you choose to be grateful? Will your thoughts and choices today be ones that you are proud of tomorrow? If you choose to be disappointed and disgruntled today how will that affect tomorrow's choices? If you choose to be happy and optimistic today how will that affect tomorrow's choices? Now – Question your thinking. Question your choices.

	QUOTE	JOURNAL PROMPT/TASK
11	Be responsible for what you are focusing on. Love & light Valerie 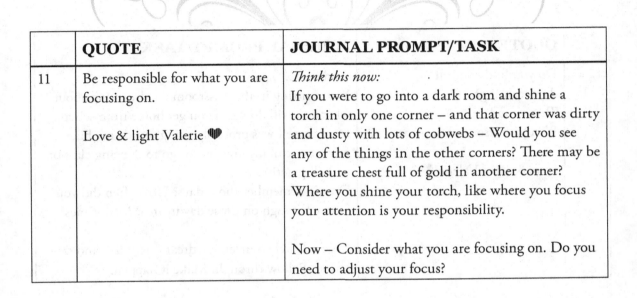	*Think this now:* If you were to go into a dark room and shine a torch in only one corner – and that corner was dirty and dusty with lots of cobwebs – Would you see any of the things in the other corners? There may be a treasure chest full of gold in another corner? Where you shine your torch, like where you focus your attention is your responsibility. Now – Consider what you are focusing on. Do you need to adjust your focus?

	QUOTE	JOURNAL PROMPT/TASK
12	Do you find yourself . daydreaming? That's good. It's a precursor to taking action. Love & light Valerie 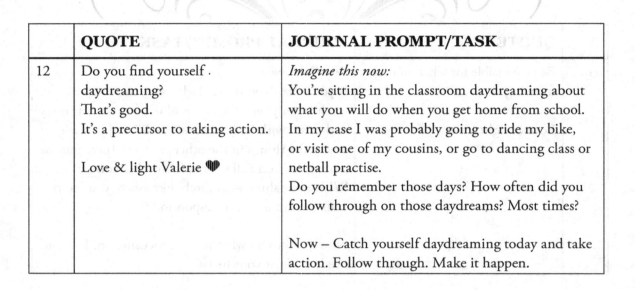	*Imagine this now:* You're sitting in the classroom daydreaming about what you will do when you get home from school. In my case I was probably going to ride my bike, or visit one of my cousins, or go to dancing class or netball practise. Do you remember those days? How often did you follow through on those daydreams? Most times? Now – Catch yourself daydreaming today and take action. Follow through. Make it happen.

	QUOTE	JOURNAL PROMPT/TASK
13	Be in awareness of everything you do. Take determined steps. What you do now will take fruition in the future. Take aware and determined steps. Love & light Valerie 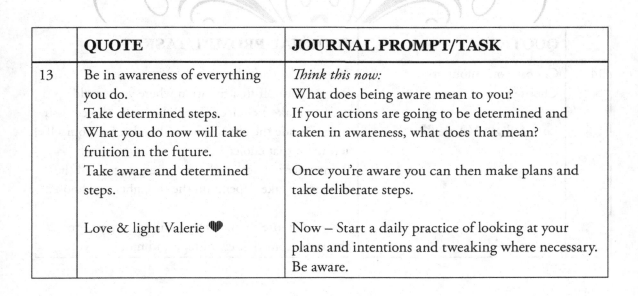	*Think this now:* What does being aware mean to you? If your actions are going to be determined and taken in awareness, what does that mean? Once you're aware you can then make plans and take deliberate steps. Now – Start a daily practice of looking at your plans and intentions and tweaking where necessary. Be aware.

	QUOTE	JOURNAL PROMPT/TASK
14	Choose your thoughts. Choose your actions. Love & light Valerie 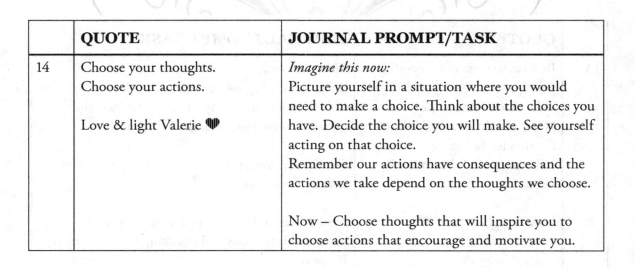	*Imagine this now:* Picture yourself in a situation where you would need to make a choice. Think about the choices you have. Decide the choice you will make. See yourself acting on that choice. Remember our actions have consequences and the actions we take depend on the thoughts we choose. Now – Choose thoughts that will inspire you to choose actions that encourage and motivate you.

	QUOTE	JOURNAL PROMPT/TASK
15	Take deliberate and intentional action towards your dreams and desires. Personal responsibility is key. Love & light Valerie 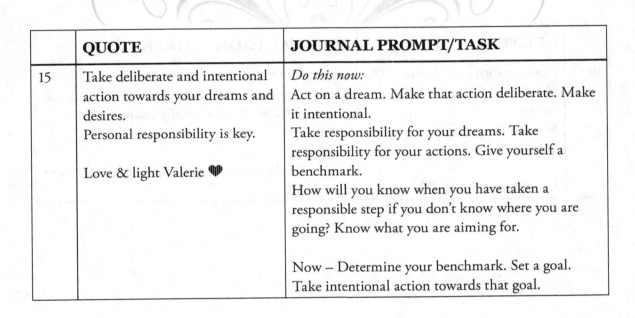	*Do this now:* Act on a dream. Make that action deliberate. Make it intentional. Take responsibility for your dreams. Take responsibility for your actions. Give yourself a benchmark. How will you know when you have taken a responsible step if you don't know where you are going? Know what you are aiming for. Now – Determine your benchmark. Set a goal. Take intentional action towards that goal.

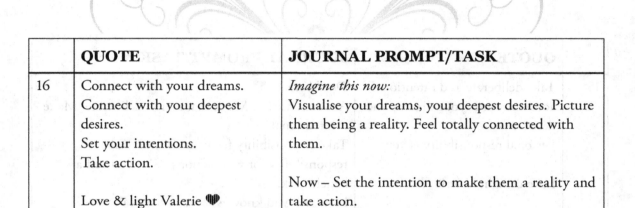

	QUOTE	JOURNAL PROMPT/TASK
16	Connect with your dreams. Connect with your deepest desires. Set your intentions. Take action. Love & light Valerie 🖤	*Imagine this now:* Visualise your dreams, your deepest desires. Picture them being a reality. Feel totally connected with them. Now – Set the intention to make them a reality and take action.

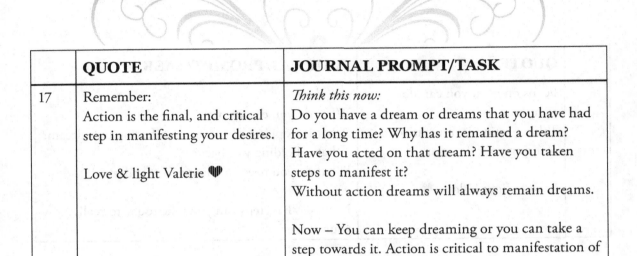

	QUOTE	JOURNAL PROMPT/TASK
17	Remember: Action is the final, and critical step in manifesting your desires. Love & light Valerie 🖤	*Think this now:* Do you have a dream or dreams that you have had for a long time? Why has it remained a dream? Have you acted on that dream? Have you taken steps to manifest it? Without action dreams will always remain dreams. Now – You can keep dreaming or you can take a step towards it. Action is critical to manifestation of any dream.

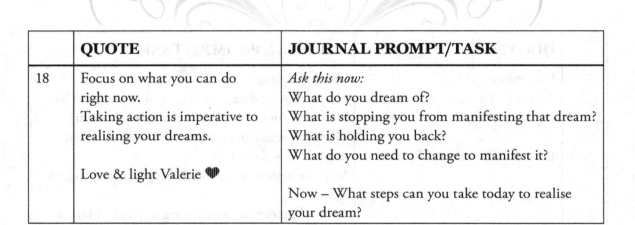

	QUOTE	JOURNAL PROMPT/TASK
18	Focus on what you can do right now. Taking action is imperative to realising your dreams. Love & light Valerie 🖤	*Ask this now:* What do you dream of? What is stopping you from manifesting that dream? What is holding you back? What do you need to change to manifest it? Now – What steps can you take today to realise your dream?

	QUOTE	JOURNAL PROMPT/TASK
19	Move about today as though every move you make and every step you take has a purpose. Love & light Valerie 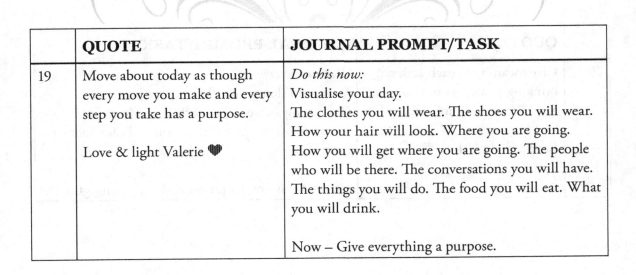	*Do this now:* Visualise your day. The clothes you will wear. The shoes you will wear. How your hair will look. Where you are going. How you will get where you are going. The people who will be there. The conversations you will have. The things you will do. The food you will eat. What you will drink. Now – Give everything a purpose.

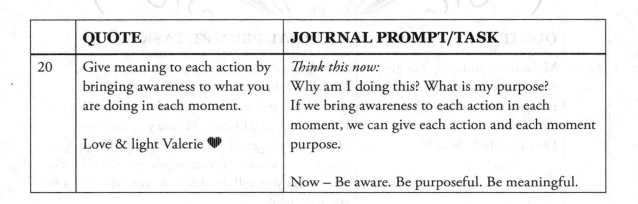

	QUOTE	JOURNAL PROMPT/TASK
20	Give meaning to each action by bringing awareness to what you are doing in each moment. Love & light Valerie ♥	*Think this now:* Why am I doing this? What is my purpose? If we bring awareness to each action in each moment, we can give each action and each moment purpose. Now – Be aware. Be purposeful. Be meaningful.

	QUOTE	JOURNAL PROMPT/TASK
21	Be the initiator. Be pro-active. Be willing to take action and to back yourself up. Love & light Valerie ♥	*Imagine this now:* You're at a meeting to discuss a new project. Everyone is present. It was supposed to start 15 minutes ago. But everyone is sitting there silent. Why? Everyone is waiting for someone else to start. What would happen if we all waited for someone else to start? Now – Be pro-active. Initiate a beginning. Back yourself.

	QUOTE	JOURNAL PROMPT/TASK
22	Pause. Make sure your actions are in alignment with your desires. Love & light Valerie	*Ask this now:* Is what I am doing in alignment with what I want? If you want to be fit and healthy and you are watching TV and eating chocolate and drinking wine your actions are not in alignment with what you say you want. Sometimes what we say we want and what we really want or are prepared to do to get it are not congruent. Now – Think about how you use your time. Can you use your time in a way that is more productive and more in alignment with your desires?

	QUOTE	JOURNAL PROMPT/TASK
23	Back up your words with your actions. Love & light Valerie 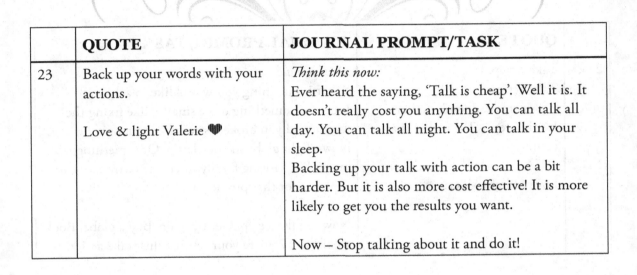	*Think this now:* Ever heard the saying, 'Talk is cheap'. Well it is. It doesn't really cost you anything. You can talk all day. You can talk all night. You can talk in your sleep. Backing up your talk with action can be a bit harder. But it is also more cost effective! It is more likely to get you the results you want. Now – Stop talking about it and do it!

	QUOTE	JOURNAL PROMPT/TASK
24	Take a step. Take action. Big or small, doesn't matter. It's the step – The action that counts. Love & light Valerie 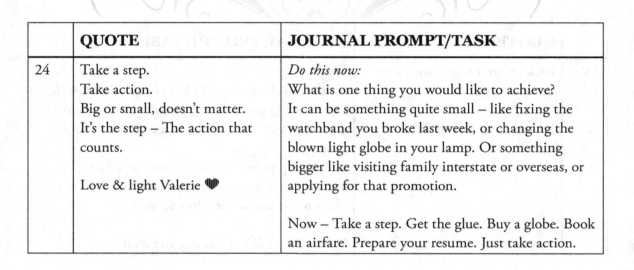	*Do this now:* What is one thing you would like to achieve? It can be something quite small – like fixing the watchband you broke last week, or changing the blown light globe in your lamp. Or something bigger like visiting family interstate or overseas, or applying for that promotion. Now – Take a step. Get the glue. Buy a globe. Book an airfare. Prepare your resume. Just take action.

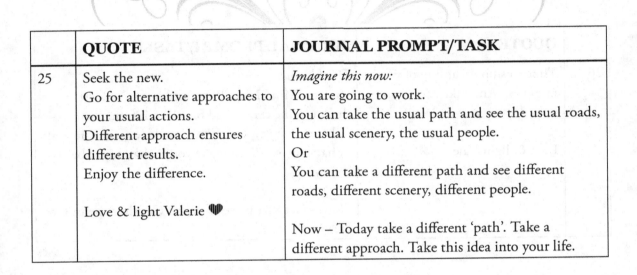

	QUOTE	JOURNAL PROMPT/TASK
25	Seek the new. Go for alternative approaches to your usual actions. Different approach ensures different results. Enjoy the difference. Love & light Valerie ♥	*Imagine this now:* You are going to work. You can take the usual path and see the usual roads, the usual scenery, the usual people. Or You can take a different path and see different roads, different scenery, different people. Now – Today take a different 'path'. Take a different approach. Take this idea into your life.

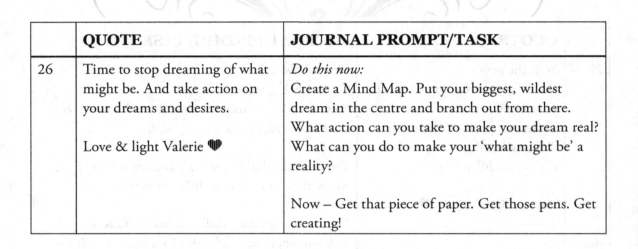

	QUOTE	JOURNAL PROMPT/TASK
26	Time to stop dreaming of what might be. And take action on your dreams and desires. Love & light Valerie ♥	*Do this now:* Create a Mind Map. Put your biggest, wildest dream in the centre and branch out from there. What action can you take to make your dream real? What can you do to make your 'what might be' a reality? Now – Get that piece of paper. Get those pens. Get creating!

	QUOTE	JOURNAL PROMPT/TASK
27	Flowers don't think and talk about flowering – they just do it. Love & light Valerie 	*Ask this now:* Are you talking about the action you 'plan' to take? Or are you taking action? Now – Be like a flower and just bloom!

	QUOTE	JOURNAL PROMPT/TASK
28	Analysis paralysis. Actions prove who you are. Words just prove who you want to be. Love & light Valerie 🖤	*Think this now:* Do you have an idea that you keep analysing? Are you gathering information about it? Are you hesitating? Are you talking about it? Thinking about it? There is often a gap between what we say we want and what we actually want and are prepared to act on. Now – What action are you prepared to take today?

	QUOTE	JOURNAL PROMPT/TASK
29	Give your ideas and dreams physical form by taking action on them. Love & light Valerie ♥	*Imagine this now:* Where would the world be if Walt Disney had never acted on his dreams? All those amazing characters and movies and Disneyland. None of it would exist if he had not taken action on his dreams and ideas. Now – What do you need to do to get your ideas and dreams into the physical world? To make them a reality? You have much to share. Share it!

3. Choose Trust Over Doubt

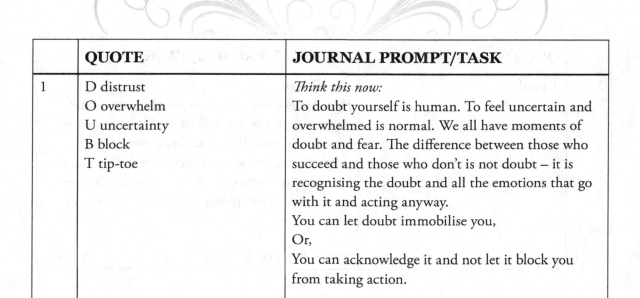

	QUOTE	JOURNAL PROMPT/TASK
1	D distrust O overwhelm U uncertainty B block T tip-toe	*Think this now:* To doubt yourself is human. To feel uncertain and overwhelmed is normal. We all have moments of doubt and fear. The difference between those who succeed and those who don't is not doubt – it is recognising the doubt and all the emotions that go with it and acting anyway. You can let doubt immobilise you, Or, You can acknowledge it and not let it block you from taking action. Now – Trust – You've got this!

	QUOTE	JOURNAL PROMPT/TASK
2	T total R response U understanding S sure T take action	*Ask this now:* How many stories have you heard of heroes and successful people that just woke up one morning having achieved all their dreams? None? Do you think they never doubted themselves? Whether we doubt or trust is our choice. Yet the results will be completely different if we choose to trust. Now – Have faith. Trust.

	QUOTE	JOURNAL PROMPT/TASK
3	Trust in your future visions. Focus on what you want more of. Be prepared to put in the daily action steps to bring it about. And trust that what comes about is for your highest good. Love & light Valerie 🖤	*Do this now:* Take some time to think about your future. Your dreams. Your hopes. Your vision for your future. Write down some goals that will help that vision become a reality. Then choose one goal and break it down into smaller goals over shorter timeframes. Now – Break those goals into daily steps. And Trust. Trust in your ability to take those daily steps.

	QUOTE	JOURNAL PROMPT/TASK
4	Don't over think. Simply take action. Trust. You know what's best for you. Love & light Valerie 🖤	*Think this now:* I had to write *think this now* because 'Don't over think' was in the quote. How many times have you thought about something and not acted until it was too late? By the time you went to purchase your ticket the event was sold out. By the time you went to put a deposit on the item someone else had already done that. When we over think it is like analysis paralysis. Deep down you always know what is best for you. Now – Stop over thinking and take action. Trust in yourself.

	QUOTE	JOURNAL PROMPT/TASK
5	Are you getting in your own way? Are you trying to control things? It's time to get out of your head and trust. You have everything you need. You can do this thing called life. Love & light Valerie 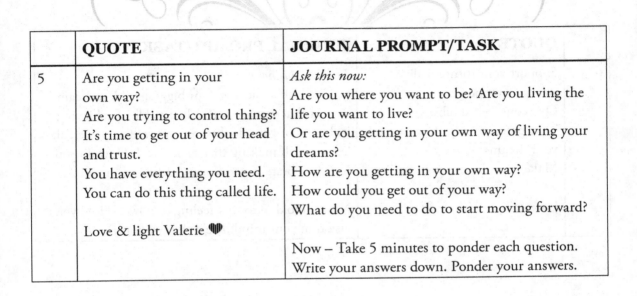	*Ask this now:* Are you where you want to be? Are you living the life you want to live? Or are you getting in your own way of living your dreams? How are you getting in your own way? How could you get out of your way? What do you need to do to start moving forward? Now – Take 5 minutes to ponder each question. Write your answers down. Ponder your answers.

	QUOTE	JOURNAL PROMPT/TASK
6	Support your future reality. Accept your power. Overcome self-doubt. Take practical steps to create your dreams. Make your dreams your reality. Love & light Valerie ♥	*Imagine this now:* See yourself achieving your biggest wildest dream. Accept that you are perfectly capable of achieving it. Let go of your doubts. See yourself as powerful. See yourself making that dream real. How do you feel? Celebrate your power. Celebrate your success. Now – Hold onto that feeling of power. Hold your vision in your mind. Meld the two together.

	QUOTE	JOURNAL PROMPT/TASK
7	The more decisions you are forced to make alone the more you become aware of your freedom to choose. Love & light Valerie 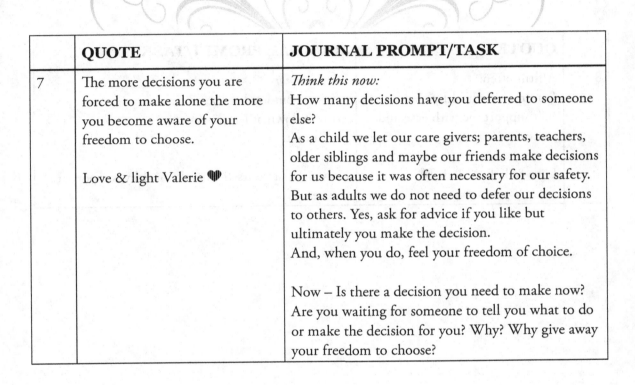	*Think this now:* How many decisions have you deferred to someone else? As a child we let our care givers; parents, teachers, older siblings and maybe our friends make decisions for us because it was often necessary for our safety. But as adults we do not need to defer our decisions to others. Yes, ask for advice if you like but ultimately you make the decision. And, when you do, feel your freedom of choice. Now – Is there a decision you need to make now? Are you waiting for someone to tell you what to do or make the decision for you? Why? Why give away your freedom to choose?

	QUOTE	JOURNAL PROMPT/TASK
8	Affirm often: I am making healthy choices that support me with ease and grace. Love & light Valerie 🖤	*Do this now:* Affirm it out loud at least 3 times. Write it down at least 3 times. Feel into it. Now – Trust yourself to make healthy, supportive choices.

	QUOTE	JOURNAL PROMPT/TASK
9	Trust your intuition and your instincts. Love & light Valerie 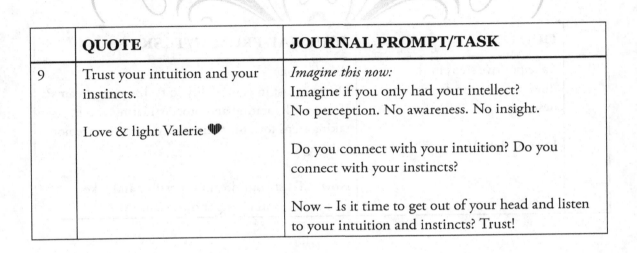	*Imagine this now:* Imagine if you only had your intellect? No perception. No awareness. No insight. Do you connect with your intuition? Do you connect with your instincts? Now – Is it time to get out of your head and listen to your intuition and instincts? Trust!

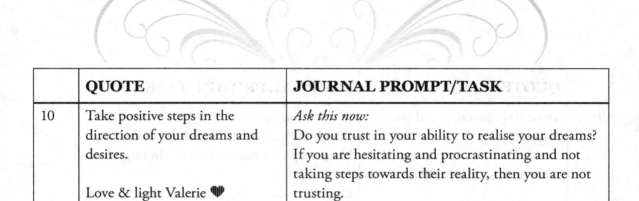

	QUOTE	JOURNAL PROMPT/TASK
10	Take positive steps in the direction of your dreams and desires. Love & light Valerie ♥	*Ask this now:* Do you trust in your ability to realise your dreams? If you are hesitating and procrastinating and not taking steps towards their reality, then you are not trusting. Now – Trust your dream is possible and take positive steps in the right direction.

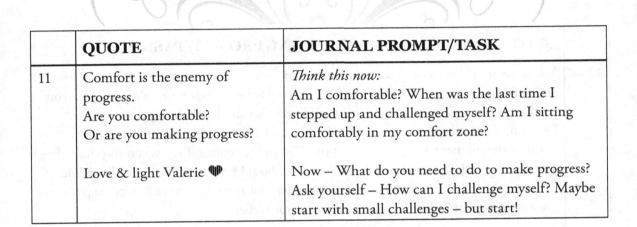

	QUOTE	JOURNAL PROMPT/TASK
11	Comfort is the enemy of progress. Are you comfortable? Or are you making progress? Love & light Valerie ♥	*Think this now:* Am I comfortable? When was the last time I stepped up and challenged myself? Am I sitting comfortably in my comfort zone? Now – What do you need to do to make progress? Ask yourself – How can I challenge myself? Maybe start with small challenges – but start!

	QUOTE	JOURNAL PROMPT/TASK
12	You came into this world open and trusting. Be that now. Be open. Be trusting. Trust in the moment. Trust in the path before you. Love & light Valerie 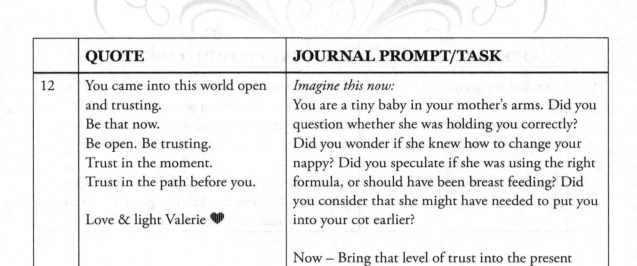	*Imagine this now:* You are a tiny baby in your mother's arms. Did you question whether she was holding you correctly? Did you wonder if she knew how to change your nappy? Did you speculate if she was using the right formula, or should have been breast feeding? Did you consider that she might have needed to put you into your cot earlier? Now – Bring that level of trust into the present moment.

	QUOTE	JOURNAL PROMPT/TASK
13	You always have two options of choice. One comes from your head and the other comes from your heart. It's your task to work these two together and thus make the wisest choices. Love & light Valerie ♥	*Ask this now:* When faced with choices do you go straight to the head, or do you use your heart, or better still, do you meld the head and the heart together to make your choice? Most of us will have a default that we are probably unaware of. Notice your preference. When we can balance using our head and heart to choose, our choices are the best and wisest ones. Now – Next time you need to make a choice, no matter how small, become aware of your process. Notice this; and bring in the other – the head or the heart. For most of us it will mean we need to bring in the heart.

	QUOTE	JOURNAL PROMPT/TASK
14	Let your doubts surface. Consider them. Then remind yourself of the bigger picture and let that buoy you up. Love & light Valerie ♥	*Think this now:* We all have doubts. We are human. Think about a dream you have. Write down all the doubts about achieving that dream: It will cost too much money, Not enough time, Too busy, It might not work, I might be rejected, I might fail. Now – Go back to your dream. See it as successful. See it happening. Let the bigger picture override the doubts.

	QUOTE	JOURNAL PROMPT/TASK
15	Trust that all is well. Trust that all is as it should be. Love & light Valerie 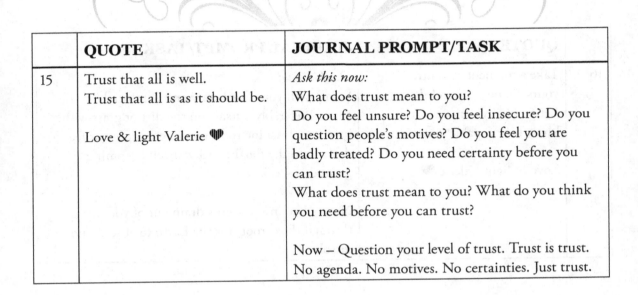	*Ask this now:* What does trust mean to you? Do you feel unsure? Do you feel insecure? Do you question people's motives? Do you feel you are badly treated? Do you need certainty before you can trust? What does trust mean to you? What do you think you need before you can trust? Now – Question your level of trust. Trust is trust. No agenda. No motives. No certainties. Just trust.

	QUOTE	JOURNAL PROMPT/TASK
16	Take a moment to centre yourself and be grateful. Let go of any concerns and know how capable you are. Love & light Valerie ♥	*Do this now:* Stand with your feet firmly and comfortably apart. Preferably outside on the dirt or grass with bare feet. Imagine roots growing out of your feet down into the Earth. Feel yourself becoming grounded – centred. Now – Let any concerns drain out of you down through those roots for the Earth to absorb and dissolve.

	QUOTE	JOURNAL PROMPT/TASK
17	Allow your doubt and resistance to propel you forward. Love & light Valerie 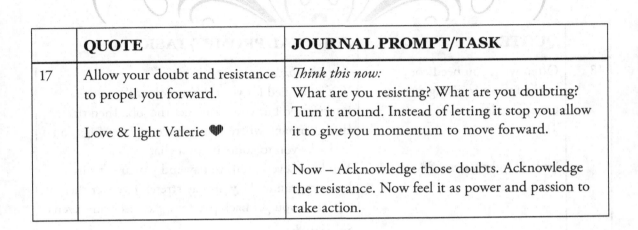	*Think this now:* What are you resisting? What are you doubting? Turn it around. Instead of letting it stop you allow it to give you momentum to move forward. Now – Acknowledge those doubts. Acknowledge the resistance. Now feel it as power and passion to take action.

	QUOTE	JOURNAL PROMPT/TASK
18	Often what you need comes in the most surprising and unexpected ways. Trust. Love & light Valerie 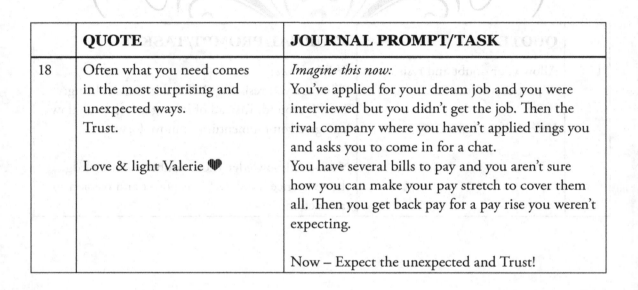	*Imagine this now:* You've applied for your dream job and you were interviewed but you didn't get the job. Then the rival company where you haven't applied rings you and asks you to come in for a chat. You have several bills to pay and you aren't sure how you can make your pay stretch to cover them all. Then you get back pay for a pay rise you weren't expecting. Now – Expect the unexpected and Trust!

	QUOTE	JOURNAL PROMPT/TASK
19	Personal trust and authenticity are calling you. Investigate your truth. Follow through on your desires. Know that you are connected with your own destiny. Love & light Valerie 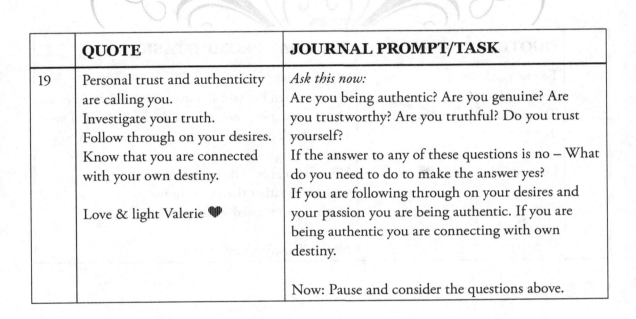	*Ask this now:* Are you being authentic? Are you genuine? Are you trustworthy? Are you truthful? Do you trust yourself? If the answer to any of these questions is no – What do you need to do to make the answer yes? If you are following through on your desires and your passion you are being authentic. If you are being authentic you are connecting with own destiny. Now: Pause and consider the questions above.

	QUOTE	JOURNAL PROMPT/TASK
20	Follow your heart. Your instincts. Try not to second guess yourself. Trust. Love & light Valerie ♥	*Ask this now:* Do you often hesitate and over think your choices? Do you question yourself and doubt yourself? Do you go back over the details trying to ensure you've made the right decision? What if you centred yourself first and listened to your heart rather than your head? What if you trusted your instincts? Now – Trust yourself.

	QUOTE	JOURNAL PROMPT/TASK
21	Notice your repetitive thoughts. Notice them. Don't judge them. What are they showing you? Love & light Valerie 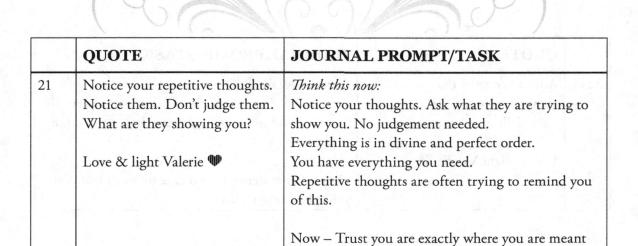	*Think this now:* Notice your thoughts. Ask what they are trying to show you. No judgement needed. Everything is in divine and perfect order. You have everything you need. Repetitive thoughts are often trying to remind you of this. Now – Trust you are exactly where you are meant to be.

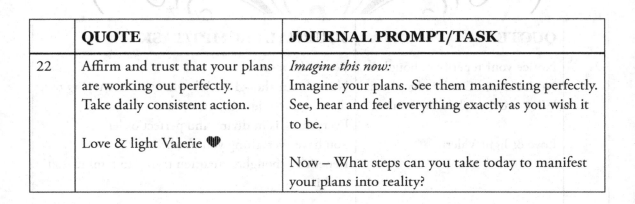

	QUOTE	JOURNAL PROMPT/TASK
22	Affirm and trust that your plans are working out perfectly. Take daily consistent action. Love & light Valerie 🖤	*Imagine this now:* Imagine your plans. See them manifesting perfectly. See, hear and feel everything exactly as you wish it to be. Now – What steps can you take today to manifest your plans into reality?

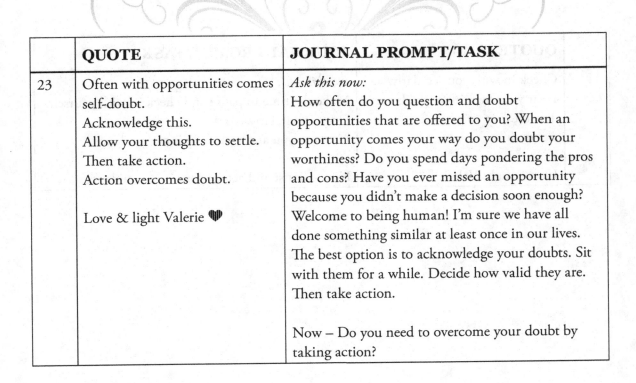

	QUOTE	JOURNAL PROMPT/TASK
23	Often with opportunities comes self-doubt. Acknowledge this. Allow your thoughts to settle. Then take action. Action overcomes doubt. Love & light Valerie	*Ask this now:* How often do you question and doubt opportunities that are offered to you? When an opportunity comes your way do you doubt your worthiness? Do you spend days pondering the pros and cons? Have you ever missed an opportunity because you didn't make a decision soon enough? Welcome to being human! I'm sure we have all done something similar at least once in our lives. The best option is to acknowledge your doubts. Sit with them for a while. Decide how valid they are. Then take action. Now – Do you need to overcome your doubt by taking action?

	QUOTE	JOURNAL PROMPT/TASK
24	Check in with you regularly. Hear your own inner guidance. Trust it. Act on it. Love & light Valerie ♥	*Do this now:* Make the time to pause and check in with yourself. Do this regularly. Listen to you and your own inner guidance. Now – Trust and act on your inner guidance.

	QUOTE	JOURNAL PROMPT/TASK
25	Remember who you are. Remember you are the one who creates your reality. Create wisely. Reveal yourself. Love & light Valerie 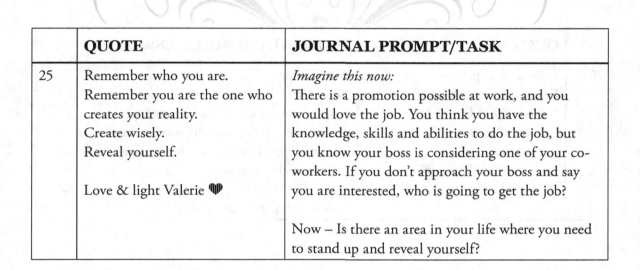	*Imagine this now:* There is a promotion possible at work, and you would love the job. You think you have the knowledge, skills and abilities to do the job, but you know your boss is considering one of your co-workers. If you don't approach your boss and say you are interested, who is going to get the job? Now – Is there an area in your life where you need to stand up and reveal yourself?

	QUOTE	JOURNAL PROMPT/TASK
26	Trust and be patient. Know that your desires are coming about for the highest good of all concerned. Love & light Valerie 🖤	*Ask this now:* Do you trust? Can you relax into an inner knowing? Or do you question and distrust at every moment? Did you know that when you are impatient it is an indication that you are not trusting? Now – Relax. Be patient. TRUST!

	QUOTE	JOURNAL PROMPT/TASK
27	Observe your life. Reflect. Allow and be still. Let go of judgement. Love & light Valerie 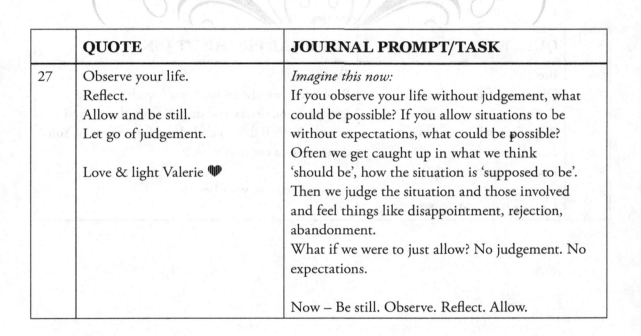	*Imagine this now:* If you observe your life without judgement, what could be possible? If you allow situations to be without expectations, what could be possible? Often we get caught up in what we think 'should be', how the situation is 'supposed to be'. Then we judge the situation and those involved and feel things like disappointment, rejection, abandonment. What if we were to just allow? No judgement. No expectations. Now – Be still. Observe. Reflect. Allow.

	QUOTE	JOURNAL PROMPT/TASK
28	Breathe. Disengage from drama and chaos. Bring yourself back to your centre. Focus on your breath. Love & light Valerie ♥	*Do this now:* Remember we always have our breath to bring us back to ourselves and detach from drama and chaos. View all drama and chaos for what it is. You don't have to connect with it. Now – Focus on your breath.

	QUOTE	JOURNAL PROMPT/TASK
29	Say and do what you mean. Come from the heart. Be true and authentic. Love & light Valerie 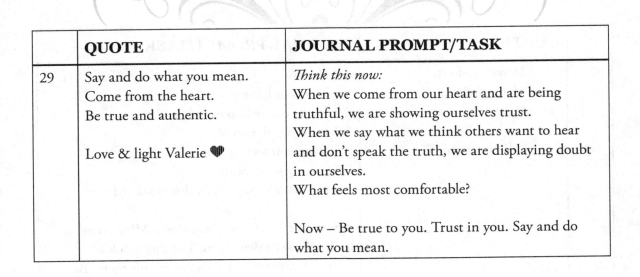	*Think this now:* When we come from our heart and are being truthful, we are showing ourselves trust. When we say what we think others want to hear and don't speak the truth, we are displaying doubt in ourselves. What feels most comfortable? Now – Be true to you. Trust in you. Say and do what you mean.

	QUOTE	JOURNAL PROMPT/TASK
30	Trust in your visions. Act with discipline. Be thorough. Love & light Valerie 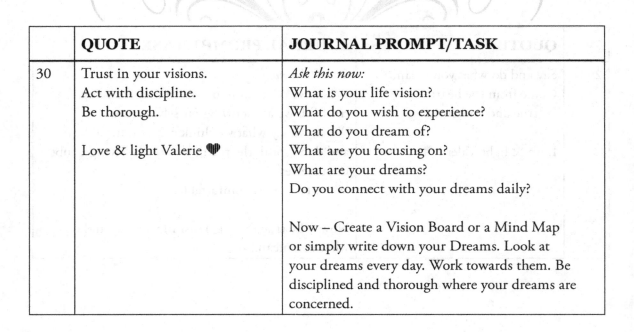	*Ask this now:* What is your life vision? What do you wish to experience? What do you dream of? What are you focusing on? What are your dreams? Do you connect with your dreams daily? Now – Create a Vision Board or a Mind Map or simply write down your Dreams. Look at your dreams every day. Work towards them. Be disciplined and thorough where your dreams are concerned.

	QUOTE	JOURNAL PROMPT/TASK
31	You have all you need within you. Believe and trust. Love & light Valerie 🖤	*Think this now:* Are you living your dreams? What is holding you back? Now – Believe and trust in you. You truly do have all you need within you.

4. Choose Clarity Over Confusion

	QUOTE	JOURNAL PROMPT/TASK
1	C complicate O options N noise F flounder U unsure S slip up I insecure O obscure N not sure	*Ask this now:* What is confusion? When do you feel confused? Do you find yourself getting confused when there are a lot of things happening around you? Or when there is a lot of noise? Or a lot of movement? Do you get confused when you go somewhere new? Now – Look at the words to the left. Does that help you realise you are normal? Confusion at times is normal. When we feel confused it can help if we stop, take a deep breath and decide what we are going to focus on.

	QUOTE	JOURNAL PROMPT/TASK
2	C clear L lucidity A alignment R reliance I intelligent T trust Y yes	*Think this now:* When you think of clarity what does that mean to you? Can you think of a time when you felt total clarity? How did it feel? What did you see? What did you hear? If asked what colour clarity was what would you answer? Is it white? Blue? Purple? Red? If asked what shape clarity was what would you answer? Is it round? Square? Triangular? Regular? Irregular? If asked what clarity sounds like what would you answer? Is it loud? Soft? Clear? Muffled? Now – Write your own definition of clarity. Write what to have clarity means to you.

	QUOTE	JOURNAL PROMPT/TASK
3	Place your focus on what will benefit you in the long term. Act in your own best interests. Love & light Valerie 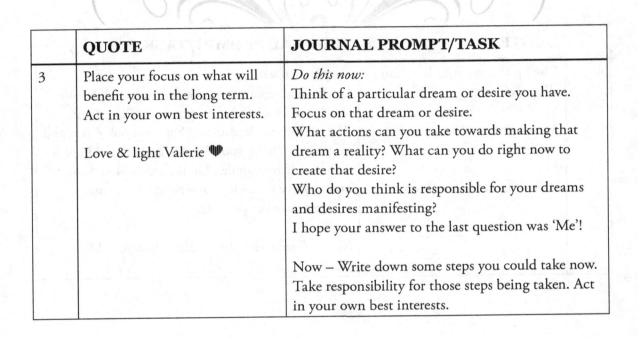	*Do this now:* Think of a particular dream or desire you have. Focus on that dream or desire. What actions can you take towards making that dream a reality? What can you do right now to create that desire? Who do you think is responsible for your dreams and desires manifesting? I hope your answer to the last question was 'Me'! Now – Write down some steps you could take now. Take responsibility for those steps being taken. Act in your own best interests.

	QUOTE	JOURNAL PROMPT/TASK
4	Rise up and see your life from all angles. See the bigger picture. Then come back down and see the now. Love & light Valerie 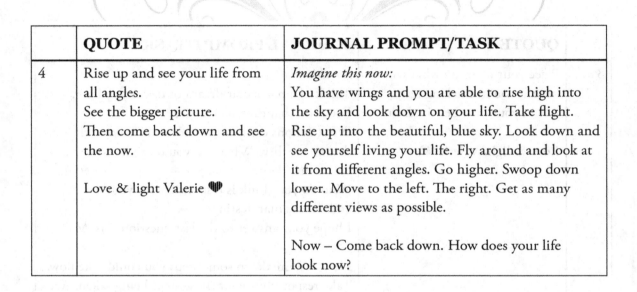	*Imagine this now:* You have wings and you are able to rise high into the sky and look down on your life. Take flight. Rise up into the beautiful, blue sky. Look down and see yourself living your life. Fly around and look at it from different angles. Go higher. Swoop down lower. Move to the left. The right. Get as many different views as possible. Now – Come back down. How does your life look now?

	QUOTE	JOURNAL PROMPT/TASK
5	You are a Soul experiencing a human life. Acknowledge this and live your life accordingly. When you come from this knowing, life can take on a whole new meaning. What meaning do you choose to give your life? Love & light Valerie 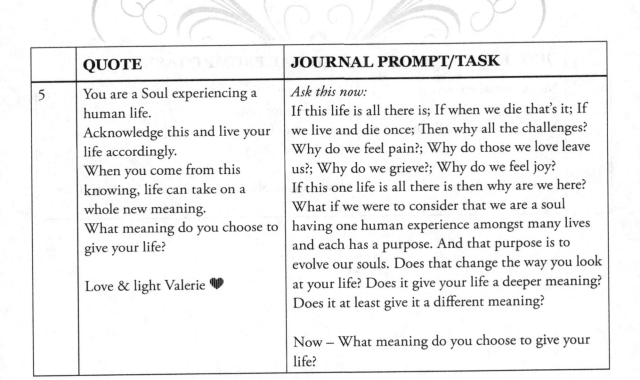	*Ask this now:* If this life is all there is; If when we die that's it; If we live and die once; Then why all the challenges? Why do we feel pain?; Why do those we love leave us?; Why do we grieve?; Why do we feel joy? If this one life is all there is then why are we here? What if we were to consider that we are a soul having one human experience amongst many lives and each has a purpose. And that purpose is to evolve our souls. Does that change the way you look at your life? Does it give your life a deeper meaning? Does it at least give it a different meaning? Now – What meaning do you choose to give your life?

	QUOTE	JOURNAL PROMPT/TASK
6	No matter where you are… Today. At least once. Make space to be still and just be. Love & light Valerie 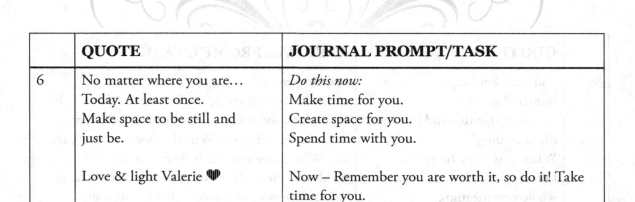	*Do this now:* Make time for you. Create space for you. Spend time with you. Now – Remember you are worth it, so do it! Take time for you.

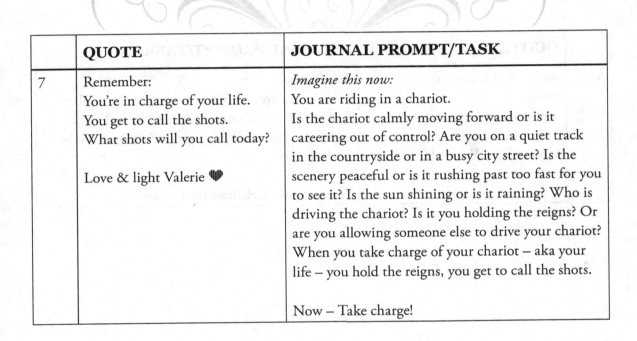

	QUOTE	JOURNAL PROMPT/TASK
7	Remember: You're in charge of your life. You get to call the shots. What shots will you call today? Love & light Valerie ♥	*Imagine this now:* You are riding in a chariot. Is the chariot calmly moving forward or is it careering out of control? Are you on a quiet track in the countryside or in a busy city street? Is the scenery peaceful or is it rushing past too fast for you to see it? Is the sun shining or is it raining? Who is driving the chariot? Is it you holding the reigns? Or are you allowing someone else to drive your chariot? When you take charge of your chariot – aka your life – you hold the reigns, you get to call the shots. Now – Take charge!

	QUOTE	JOURNAL PROMPT/TASK
8	Accept and enjoy every life moment. See every moment as a victory. Love & light Valerie ♥	*Do this now:* In each and every moment we have a choice about how we see that moment and how we feel about it. See each moment as a victory. A moment to be celebrated. Now – Smile! Celebrate the moment!

	QUOTE	JOURNAL PROMPT/TASK
9	Create opportunities. Rather than wait for circumstances to change. Create your own change. Love & light Valerie 🖤	*Think this now:* How often have you been wishing and hoping for something to happen, something to change and then you have missed an opportunity? How often has an opportunity passed you by? We need to create our own opportunities. If we just wait for things to change, they could change, and they will change – as change is inevitable, but the changes won't necessarily be what you wished and hoped for. Now – Create the change you wish to see.

	QUOTE	JOURNAL PROMPT/TASK
10	You choose how you will see, hear and experience life, by how you look at and approach life. What perspective will you choose today? Love & light Valerie 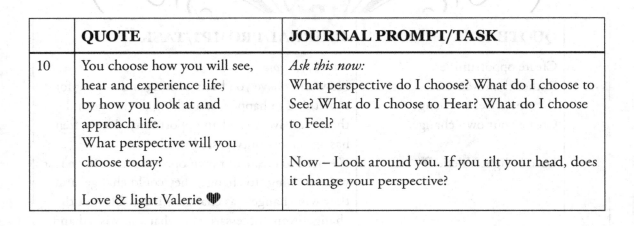	*Ask this now:* What perspective do I choose? What do I choose to See? What do I choose to Hear? What do I choose to Feel? Now – Look around you. If you tilt your head, does it change your perspective?

	QUOTE	JOURNAL PROMPT/TASK
11	If circumstances push your buttons. Pause - before you decide and act. Love & light Valerie 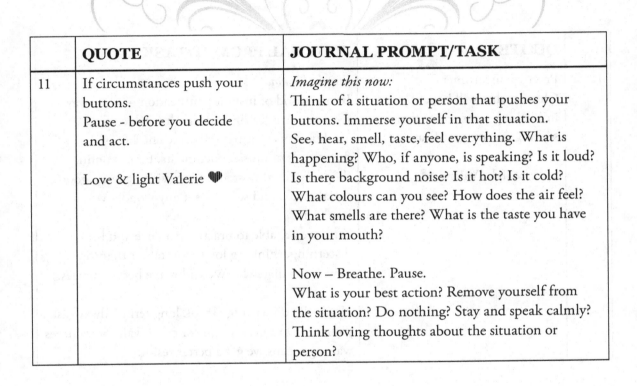	*Imagine this now:* Think of a situation or person that pushes your buttons. Immerse yourself in that situation. See, hear, smell, taste, feel everything. What is happening? Who, if anyone, is speaking? Is it loud? Is there background noise? Is it hot? Is it cold? What colours can you see? How does the air feel? What smells are there? What is the taste you have in your mouth? Now – Breathe. Pause. What is your best action? Remove yourself from the situation? Do nothing? Stay and speak calmly? Think loving thoughts about the situation or person?

	QUOTE	JOURNAL PROMPT/TASK
12	Practice discernment. Choose what will benefit you in the long term rather than seeking instant gratification. Love & light Valerie ♥	*Think this now:* In our world of instant gratification – take-away food and drinks; drive through food, coffee, alcohol, dry cleaning; self-serve checkouts; downloads of music, documents, books; online shopping for almost anything; video games; google; social media and so on –Is it any wonder we are impatient? Yet if we are able to practise patience and be discerning, thinking long term rather than right now, immediately! – We will make better choices. Now – Be discerning. Think long term. Always ask yourself. Do I need it now or can I wait? Sometimes waiting means we get a better result.

	QUOTE	JOURNAL PROMPT/TASK
13	Listen to others' stories rather than telling your own. Love & light Valerie 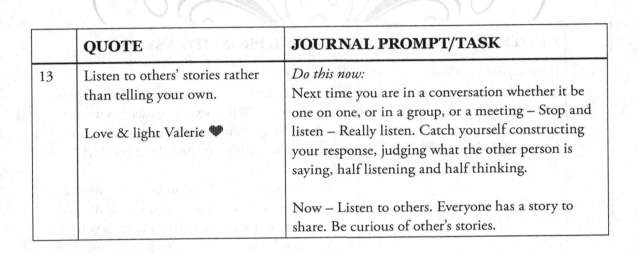	*Do this now:* Next time you are in a conversation whether it be one on one, or in a group, or a meeting – Stop and listen – Really listen. Catch yourself constructing your response, judging what the other person is saying, half listening and half thinking. Now – Listen to others. Everyone has a story to share. Be curious of other's stories.

	QUOTE	JOURNAL PROMPT/TASK
14	Initiate your own way. Move where your heart takes you. Love & light Valerie 🖤	*Ask this now:* Where do you want to be? Where do you feel you are meant to be? What is your passion? What makes your heart 'sing'? What would make you want to wake up each morning excited about the day? Now – Initiate. Create a Vision Board, or write a Wish List, or write down your goals. And display it where you will see it every day. Put it on your bathroom mirror, your fridge, your car dashboard, your bedroom cupboard door. Make it your phone background. Just put it somewhere you will look at it daily. And do just that! Look at it daily. Read it daily!

	QUOTE	JOURNAL PROMPT/TASK
15	Check in. Be still and reflect. Love & light Valerie ♥	*Do this now:* Pause and be still. Take a deep breath in through the nose and out through the mouth. Reflect. Check in with you. How are you feeling? Do you need to think about why you are feeling that way? Would it be helpful to change how you feel? Now – Check in with you.

	QUOTE	JOURNAL PROMPT/TASK
16	Envision your ideal life. AND take the steps necessary for it to become your reality. Love & light Valerie 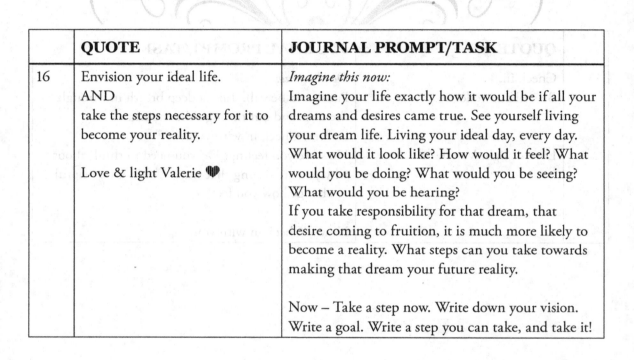	*Imagine this now:* Imagine your life exactly how it would be if all your dreams and desires came true. See yourself living your dream life. Living your ideal day, every day. What would it look like? How would it feel? What would you be doing? What would you be seeing? What would you be hearing? If you take responsibility for that dream, that desire coming to fruition, it is much more likely to become a reality. What steps can you take towards making that dream your future reality. Now – Take a step now. Write down your vision. Write a goal. Write a step you can take, and take it!

	QUOTE	JOURNAL PROMPT/TASK
17	Pause often. Allow yourself to regroup. Love & light Valerie ♥	*Think this now:* Pausing and allowing yourself to regroup gives you time to think. It gives you the space to consider if there are other options and possibilities. Become aware and pause and gift yourself this opportunity. Now – Pause! Regroup.

	QUOTE	JOURNAL PROMPT/TASK
18	Set your intentions. Your priorities determine your outcomes. Love & light Valerie ♥	*Imagine this now:* You are in a car driving on the freeway. You've been driving for a long time. You have passed several exits. You considered taking some of them but you're not sure where you are going, so you don't know which exit to take. Or You are in your car driving on the freeway and you set the intention before you left home of your destination. You know the exit you need is just ahead of you, and you will go off there and take the first road to your right. Shortly after that you will arrive at your desired destination. Now – If you know your intentions you can prioritise which exit to take – which path to take – and you can determine your destination – your outcome.

	QUOTE	JOURNAL PROMPT/TASK
19	When your thoughts race, be aware. By being aware you can calm yourself down. Decide what is important and what needs your attention. Let the rest go. Love & light Valerie 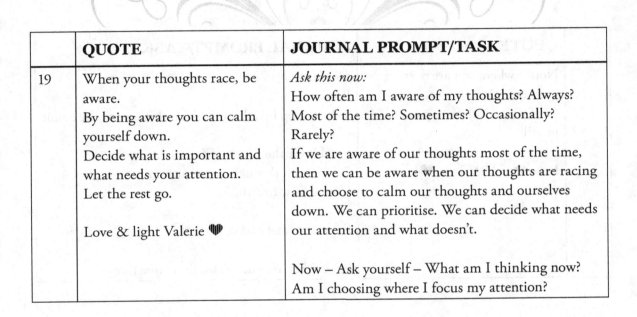	*Ask this now:* How often am I aware of my thoughts? Always? Most of the time? Sometimes? Occasionally? Rarely? If we are aware of our thoughts most of the time, then we can be aware when our thoughts are racing and choose to calm our thoughts and ourselves down. We can prioritise. We can decide what needs our attention and what doesn't. Now – Ask yourself – What am I thinking now? Am I choosing where I focus my attention?

	QUOTE	JOURNAL PROMPT/TASK
20	Notice where you are putting your attention. Give yourself time to pause and be still. Love & light Valerie 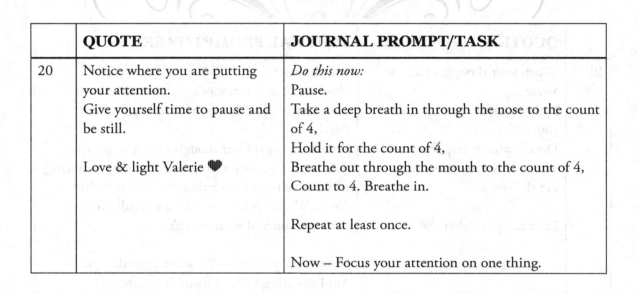	*Do this now:* Pause. Take a deep breath in through the nose to the count of 4, Hold it for the count of 4, Breathe out through the mouth to the count of 4, Count to 4. Breathe in. Repeat at least once. Now – Focus your attention on one thing.

	QUOTE	JOURNAL PROMPT/TASK
21	See past surface level illusions. Allow yourself to dig deeper. Feel your fears. Face your fears. Love & light Valerie ♥	*Ask this now:* What is my deepest fear? Is it being alone? Having no money? Being laughed at? Failing at school or work? Ill health? Is that the real fear? Or does it go deeper? Ask: Am I alone? Why do I fear being alone? Why does the idea of being alone frighten me? Do I have money? Why do fear having none? What would be the worst-case scenario? What would happen if I was laughed at? What would <u>really</u> happen? What if I failed one test at school? Or failed to get one project in on time at work? Could I have another try? Have I been sick before? What happened? Did I get better? Now – Keep asking yourself these types of questions until you get to the deeper fear. All fears are based on our fear of not being good enough; not being worthy. Who is judging you to be not good enough or unworthy? Is it you?

	QUOTE	JOURNAL PROMPT/TASK
22	Own your own choices. Take responsibility for your behaviour. Love & light Valerie ♥	*Think this now:* Choices? Decisions? How many do we make every day? We make choices and decisions constantly every day. Shall I get up now or hit snooze once more? Will I shower first or eat breakfast first? What will I wear? What will I eat? Which way will I go to work/my appointment etc.? If your past choices have got you where you are today? What will you choose today? Now – Ask this – If you are not responsible for your choices and behaviour, then who is?

	QUOTE	JOURNAL PROMPT/TASK
23	Ground yourself in each moment. Let go of over-analysing. Let go of impatience. Trust that everything is happening as it is meant to. You are where you are meant to be. Love & light Valerie ♥	*Imagine this now:* You are going on holiday. You could analyse all possibilities and plan for every eventuality before you leave home, but there will still be the possibility that there will be something you have not thought of. It could be a problem, or it may not be. Or; You could make the essential bookings pack your bags and leave home trusting that all is going to be fine. I knew someone who took a holiday flipping a coin at every intersection they came to. And they had a marvellous time exploring parts of the country they had never seen before. Now – You don't need to go on a holiday to trust that you are where you are meant to be.

	QUOTE	JOURNAL PROMPT/TASK
24	Be aware in the moment. Observe rather than think and analyse. Love & light Valerie ♥	*Do this now:* Be aware of your surroundings. What can you see, hear, feel, smell, taste? Observe the sights, the sounds, the air around you, the feel of what you are wearing, the smells, the taste in your mouth. Just observe. No need to analyse. Now – Just observe. And enjoy your surroundings.

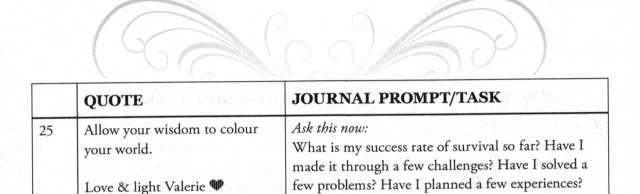

	QUOTE	JOURNAL PROMPT/TASK
25	Allow your wisdom to colour your world. Love & light Valerie 🖤	*Ask this now:* What is my success rate of survival so far? Have I made it through a few challenges? Have I solved a few problems? Have I planned a few experiences? Have I survived every day? Now – Colour your days with the wisdom of that knowing?

	QUOTE	JOURNAL PROMPT/TASK
26	Many of us are looking for certainty. Yet the only certainty in life is that life is uncertain. Embrace change and uncertainty and thus create your own certainty. Love & light Valerie 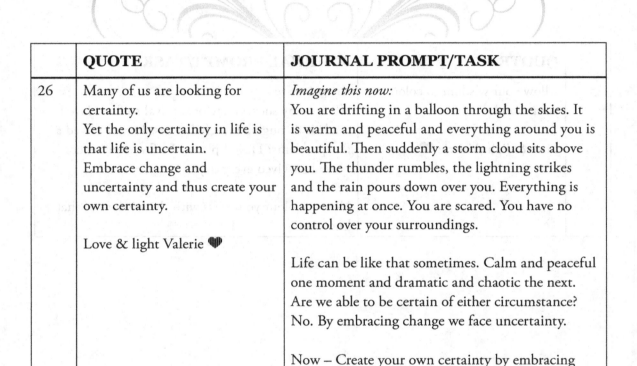	*Imagine this now:* You are drifting in a balloon through the skies. It is warm and peaceful and everything around you is beautiful. Then suddenly a storm cloud sits above you. The thunder rumbles, the lightning strikes and the rain pours down over you. Everything is happening at once. You are scared. You have no control over your surroundings. Life can be like that sometimes. Calm and peaceful one moment and dramatic and chaotic the next. Are we able to be certain of either circumstance? No. By embracing change we face uncertainty. Now – Create your own certainty by embracing change.

	QUOTE	JOURNAL PROMPT/TASK
27	How you feel each moment is your choice. How you react to each moment is your choice. Love & light Valerie 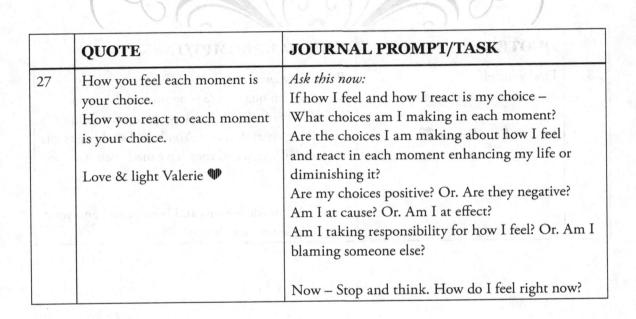	*Ask this now:* If how I feel and how I react is my choice – What choices am I making in each moment? Are the choices I am making about how I feel and react in each moment enhancing my life or diminishing it? Are my choices positive? Or. Are they negative? Am I at cause? Or. Am I at effect? Am I taking responsibility for how I feel? Or. Am I blaming someone else? Now – Stop and think. How do I feel right now?

	QUOTE	JOURNAL PROMPT/TASK
28	Find yourself. Find your own unique way. Love & light Valerie 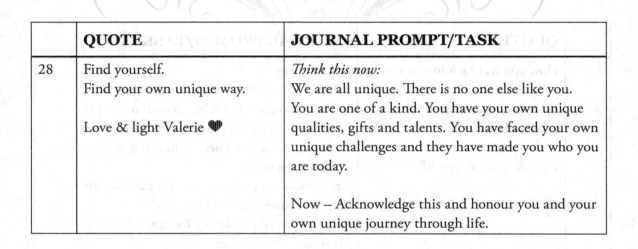	*Think this now:* We are all unique. There is no one else like you. You are one of a kind. You have your own unique qualities, gifts and talents. You have faced your own unique challenges and they have made you who you are today. Now – Acknowledge this and honour you and your own unique journey through life.

	QUOTE	JOURNAL PROMPT/TASK
29	You choose your thoughts. You choose your actions. Thus, You choose your results or consequences. Love & light Valerie 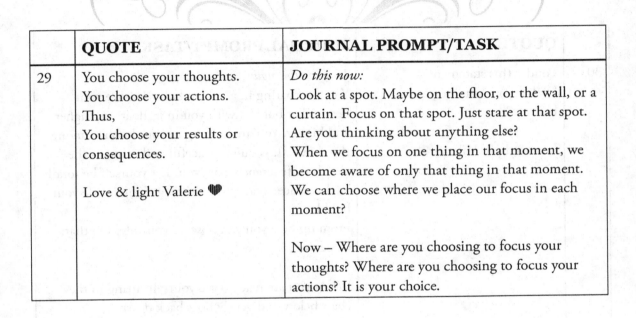	*Do this now:* Look at a spot. Maybe on the floor, or the wall, or a curtain. Focus on that spot. Just stare at that spot. Are you thinking about anything else? When we focus on one thing in that moment, we become aware of only that thing in that moment. We can choose where we place our focus in each moment? Now – Where are you choosing to focus your thoughts? Where are you choosing to focus your actions? It is your choice.

	QUOTE	JOURNAL PROMPT/TASK
30	Ponder this statement. "What you imagine you become." Love & light Valerie ♥	*Imagine this now:* You are floating in a golden bubble above your head. That bubble, with you in it, floats up higher and higher. You are floating in your bubble amongst the clouds. It is quiet, peaceful and calm, as the clouds drift serenely past you. Let yourself be totally in this space. Tranquilly drifting along inside your bubble. From up here you can observe your life. Do that. Observe. Imagine. When you are ready – see yourself sitting in the chair below and gently float back down. Take a deep breath and open your eyes. Now – Sit in that peace for a moment before you do anything else.

5. Choose Joy Over Sadness

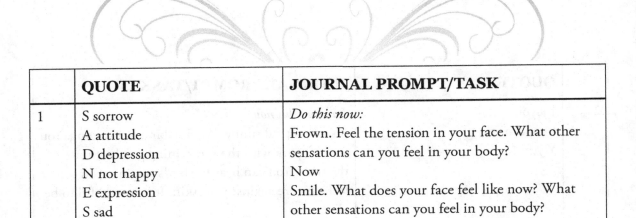

	QUOTE	JOURNAL PROMPT/TASK
1	S sorrow A attitude D depression N not happy E expression S sad S suffering	*Do this now:* Frown. Feel the tension in your face. What other sensations can you feel in your body? Now Smile. What does your face feel like now? What other sensations can you feel in your body? Now – Which expression makes you feel the best?

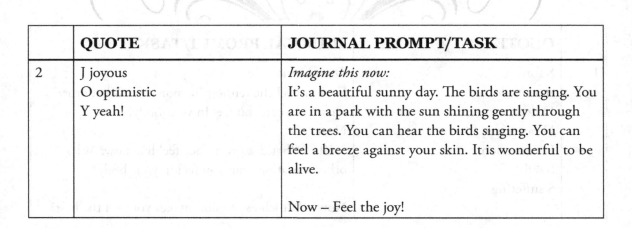

	QUOTE	JOURNAL PROMPT/TASK
2	J joyous O optimistic Y yeah!	*Imagine this now:* It's a beautiful sunny day. The birds are singing. You are in a park with the sun shining gently through the trees. You can hear the birds singing. You can feel a breeze against your skin. It is wonderful to be alive. Now – Feel the joy!

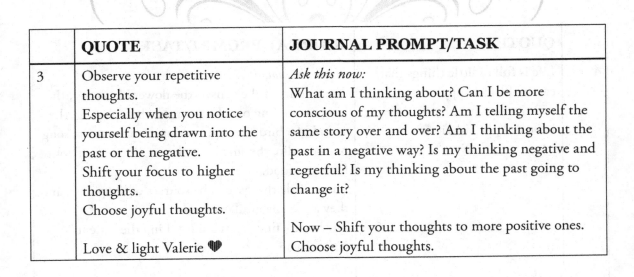

	QUOTE	JOURNAL PROMPT/TASK
3	Observe your repetitive thoughts. Especially when you notice yourself being drawn into the past or the negative. Shift your focus to higher thoughts. Choose joyful thoughts. Love & light Valerie ♥	*Ask this now:* What am I thinking about? Can I be more conscious of my thoughts? Am I telling myself the same story over and over? Am I thinking about the past in a negative way? Is my thinking negative and regretful? Is my thinking about the past going to change it? Now – Shift your thoughts to more positive ones. Choose joyful thoughts.

	QUOTE	JOURNAL PROMPT/TASK
4	Life is full of little things that can make us happy. Love & light Valerie 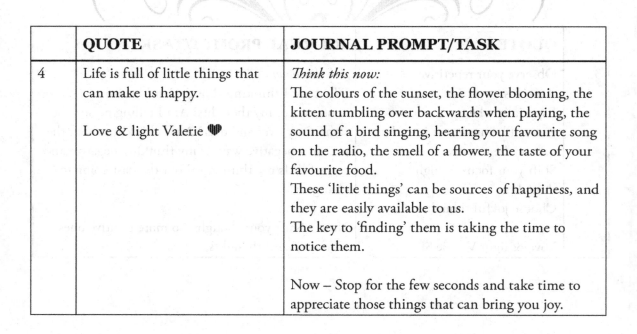	*Think this now:* The colours of the sunset, the flower blooming, the kitten tumbling over backwards when playing, the sound of a bird singing, hearing your favourite song on the radio, the smell of a flower, the taste of your favourite food. These 'little things' can be sources of happiness, and they are easily available to us. The key to 'finding' them is taking the time to notice them. Now – Stop for the few seconds and take time to appreciate those things that can bring you joy.

	QUOTE	JOURNAL PROMPT/TASK
5	Be the observer. Observe your emotions. Don't identify with them. Know the difference. Love & light Valerie 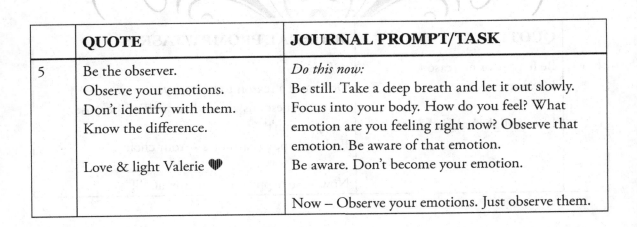	*Do this now:* Be still. Take a deep breath and let it out slowly. Focus into your body. How do you feel? What emotion are you feeling right now? Observe that emotion. Be aware of that emotion. Be aware. Don't become your emotion. Now – Observe your emotions. Just observe them.

	QUOTE	JOURNAL PROMPT/TASK
6	Be happy for no reason. It's your choice. Love & light Valerie 	*Ask this now:* Do I need a reason to be happy? No is the best answer to that question because – No, you don't! Feeling happy is a choice – Your choice. Now – Be happy for no reason at all!

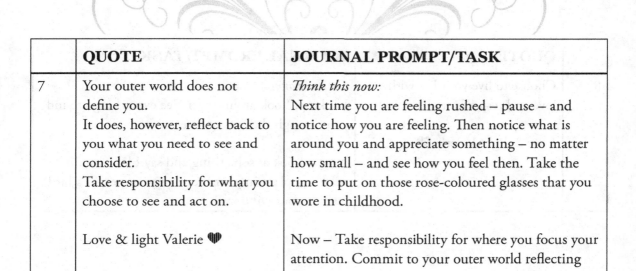

	QUOTE	JOURNAL PROMPT/TASK
7	Your outer world does not define you. It does, however, reflect back to you what you need to see and consider. Take responsibility for what you choose to see and act on. Love & light Valerie	*Think this now:* Next time you are feeling rushed – pause – and notice how you are feeling. Then notice what is around you and appreciate something – no matter how small – and see how you feel then. Take the time to put on those rose-coloured glasses that you wore in childhood. Now – Take responsibility for where you focus your attention. Commit to your outer world reflecting joy back you.

	QUOTE	JOURNAL PROMPT/TASK
8	Choose to live your life with love and respect for all. Love & light Valerie 🖤	*Do this now:* Look up. Look around you. See everything around you through the eyes of love. Now – Look at something and say I love you. It may be a plant in your room, or your pet, or a bird outside your window.

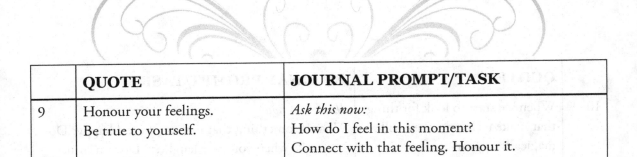

	QUOTE	JOURNAL PROMPT/TASK
9	Honour your feelings. Be true to yourself. Love & light Valerie 🖤	*Ask this now:* How do I feel in this moment? Connect with that feeling. Honour it. Now – In each moment honour how you feel.

	QUOTE	JOURNAL PROMPT/TASK
10	When we start to look for things that make us happy. they will magically appear. Love & light Valerie 🖤	*Think this now:* What is something that makes you feel happy? Do you smile when you hear laughter? Do you smile when you see a puppy chasing its tail? Do you smile when you see kittens playing? Do you smile when you eat your favourite ice-cream flavour? Now – Keep thinking of and looking for things that make you smile. The more you seek them the more they will magically appear.

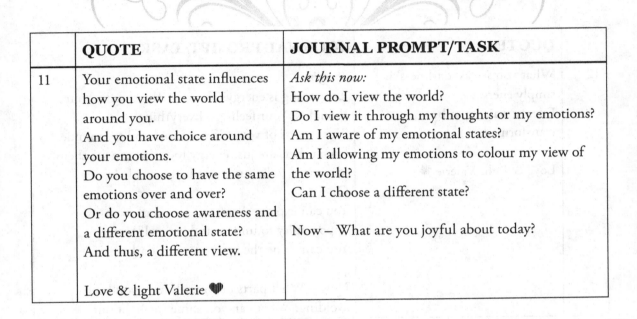

	QUOTE	JOURNAL PROMPT/TASK
11	Your emotional state influences how you view the world around you. And you have choice around your emotions. Do you choose to have the same emotions over and over? Or do you choose awareness and a different emotional state? And thus, a different view. Love & light Valerie 🖤	*Ask this now:* How do I view the world? Do I view it through my thoughts or my emotions? Am I aware of my emotional states? Am I allowing my emotions to colour my view of the world? Can I choose a different state? Now – What are you joyful about today?

	QUOTE	JOURNAL PROMPT/TASK
12	What you see as 'darkness' is simply energy. Energy waiting to be transformed. Love & light Valerie 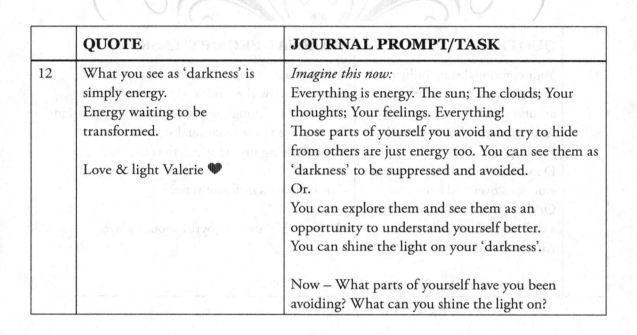	*Imagine this now:* Everything is energy. The sun; The clouds; Your thoughts; Your feelings. Everything! Those parts of yourself you avoid and try to hide from others are just energy too. You can see them as 'darkness' to be suppressed and avoided. Or. You can explore them and see them as an opportunity to understand yourself better. You can shine the light on your 'darkness'. Now – What parts of yourself have you been avoiding? What can you shine the light on?

	QUOTE	JOURNAL PROMPT/TASK
13	Focus on the love that you are — and share it! Love & light Valerie 🖤	*Think this now:* All there is — is love! If love is all there is, you must be love too! Now — Share your love.

	QUOTE	JOURNAL PROMPT/TASK
14	Do you watch children playing? Do you dance to your favourite song? Do you sing along to your favourite song? Do you savour your first mouthful of coffee in the morning? Do you watch the bees dance around the flower? Do you listen to the birds chirping? Love & light Valerie 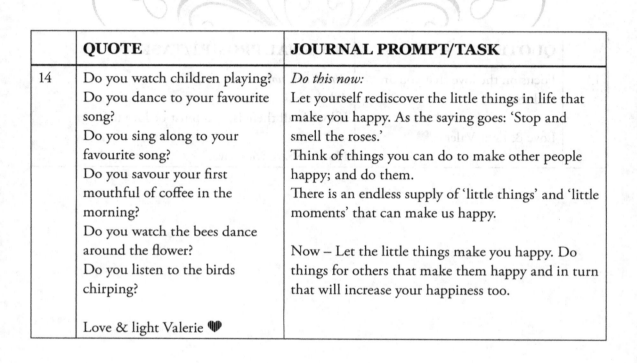	*Do this now:* Let yourself rediscover the little things in life that make you happy. As the saying goes: 'Stop and smell the roses.' Think of things you can do to make other people happy; and do them. There is an endless supply of 'little things' and 'little moments' that can make us happy. Now – Let the little things make you happy. Do things for others that make them happy and in turn that will increase your happiness too.

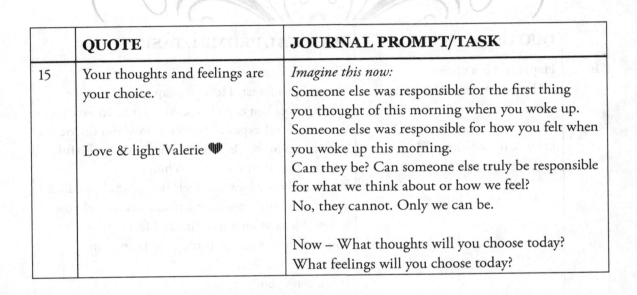

	QUOTE	JOURNAL PROMPT/TASK
15	Your thoughts and feelings are your choice. Love & light Valerie 🖤	*Imagine this now:* Someone else was responsible for the first thing you thought of this morning when you woke up. Someone else was responsible for how you felt when you woke up this morning. Can they be? Can someone else truly be responsible for what we think about or how we feel? No, they cannot. Only we can be. Now – What thoughts will you choose today? What feelings will you choose today?

	QUOTE	JOURNAL PROMPT/TASK
16	Happiness is a choice. A choice we can make at any time. Love & light Valerie ♥	*Think this now:* You are in a forest. How you experience this is your choice. You can choose to see it as an exciting adventure and explore the forest floor and the trees and the animals. Or you can choose to be fearful and panic and run and try to hide. You can choose how you feel? It is your choice how your feel at any time in any place. You can choose to see things as an adventure and feel happy? Or you can choose to see things as a disaster and feel sad? It is always your choice. Now – What do you choose?

	QUOTE	JOURNAL PROMPT/TASK
17	Joy ultimately comes from within. Allow yourself to feel that joy. Love & light Valerie 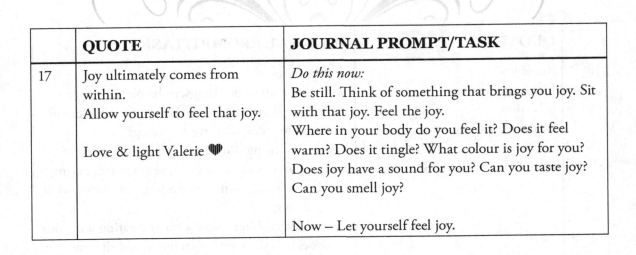	*Do this now:* Be still. Think of something that brings you joy. Sit with that joy. Feel the joy. Where in your body do you feel it? Does it feel warm? Does it tingle? What colour is joy for you? Does joy have a sound for you? Can you taste joy? Can you smell joy? Now – Let yourself feel joy.

	QUOTE	JOURNAL PROMPT/TASK
18	Remember: Life is not a race. Slow down. Be conscious. Love & light Valerie 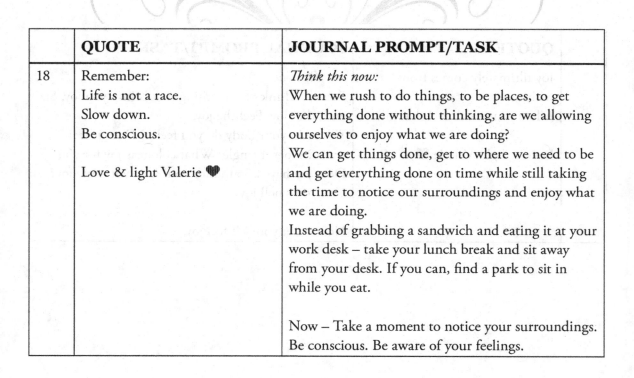	*Think this now:* When we rush to do things, to be places, to get everything done without thinking, are we allowing ourselves to enjoy what we are doing? We can get things done, get to where we need to be and get everything done on time while still taking the time to notice our surroundings and enjoy what we are doing. Instead of grabbing a sandwich and eating it at your work desk – take your lunch break and sit away from your desk. If you can, find a park to sit in while you eat. Now – Take a moment to notice your surroundings. Be conscious. Be aware of your feelings.

	QUOTE	JOURNAL PROMPT/TASK
19	You are not your emotions. You choose how you feel about what happens in your life. Let your emotions be part of you. Not you. Love & light Valerie ♥	*Imagine this now:* You are in a crowded supermarket and you are queued at the checkout. Someone comes up behind you and rams into you with their trolley, hurting your hip and leg, and they make no attempt to apologise. Most people would feel angry. It is natural to feel angry. If you feel angry and point out politely to them that it hurt and you would like an apology, you may get one. If you let the anger you feel take over and you identify with it, you will most likely react to them angrily and possibly start a fight. The difference is – In the first situation you allow yourself to feel angry and you respond asking for an apology. In the second situation you let your anger become you and you react rather than respond. Now – Which do you choose? To feel your emotions or let your emotions become you.

	QUOTE	JOURNAL PROMPT/TASK
20	Follow your heart. Do what you love. Do what makes your heart sing. Love & light Valerie 🖤	*Ask this now:* What brings me joy? What do I love to do? What makes me want to sing with joy? Now – Follow your heart.

	QUOTE	JOURNAL PROMPT/TASK
21	How you choose to live your life each day is your choice. Choose to accept your choices. Choose to enjoy each day. Love & light Valerie 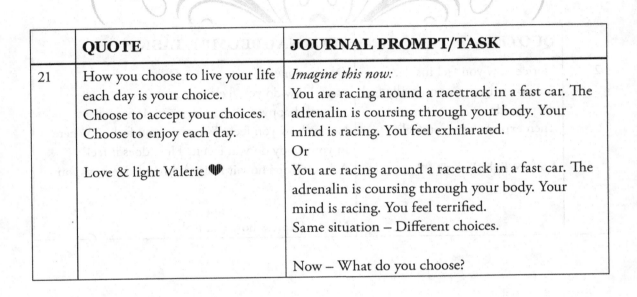	*Imagine this now:* You are racing around a racetrack in a fast car. The adrenalin is coursing through your body. Your mind is racing. You feel exhilarated. Or You are racing around a racetrack in a fast car. The adrenalin is coursing through your body. Your mind is racing. You feel terrified. Same situation – Different choices. Now – What do you choose?

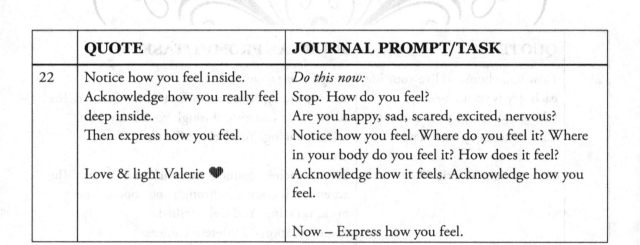

	QUOTE	JOURNAL PROMPT/TASK
22	Notice how you feel inside. Acknowledge how you really feel deep inside. Then express how you feel. Love & light Valerie ♥	*Do this now:* Stop. How do you feel? Are you happy, sad, scared, excited, nervous? Notice how you feel. Where do you feel it? Where in your body do you feel it? How does it feel? Acknowledge how it feels. Acknowledge how you feel. Now – Express how you feel.

	QUOTE	JOURNAL PROMPT/TASK
23	When you love yourself, You can extend your love out into your relationships. Love & light Valerie 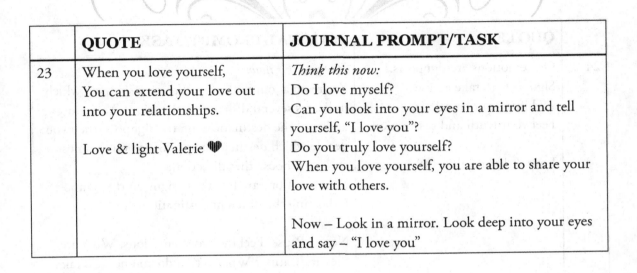	*Think this now:* Do I love myself? Can you look into your eyes in a mirror and tell yourself, "I love you"? Do you truly love yourself? When you love yourself, you are able to share your love with others. Now – Look in a mirror. Look deep into your eyes and say – "I love you"

	QUOTE	JOURNAL PROMPT/TASK
24	Our emotions are signposts. Signposts to take action. Feel into your emotions. Feel your truth and take action. Love & light Valerie ♥	*Imagine this now:* You're on a journey and you reach a signpost which indicates several different destinations. You pause and read the destinations on the signpost, then you decide which destination appeals to you the most and you choose that direction. Your emotions are like those signs on the signpost indicating the different destinations. Now – Pause. Feel into your emotions. What are they indicating? What action do you need to take to honour your emotions?

	QUOTE	JOURNAL PROMPT/TASK
25	Listen to your own advice and follow it. Love & light Valerie ♥	*Ask this now:* What advice would I give someone else right now? Would I benefit from taking that advice myself? Is there something I could change? Is there something I can do? Now – Listen to yourself. Take your own advice.

	QUOTE	JOURNAL PROMPT/TASK
26	Sink into every moment and enjoy it. Love & light Valerie 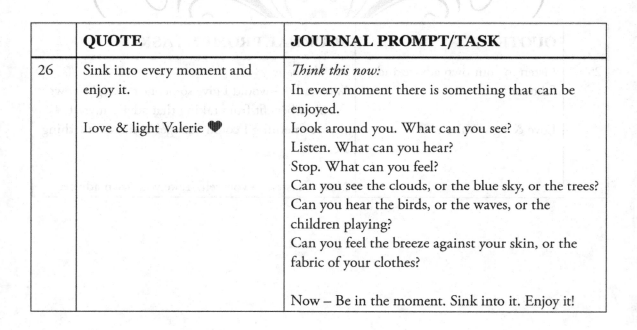	*Think this now:* In every moment there is something that can be enjoyed. Look around you. What can you see? Listen. What can you hear? Stop. What can you feel? Can you see the clouds, or the blue sky, or the trees? Can you hear the birds, or the waves, or the children playing? Can you feel the breeze against your skin, or the fabric of your clothes? Now – Be in the moment. Sink into it. Enjoy it!

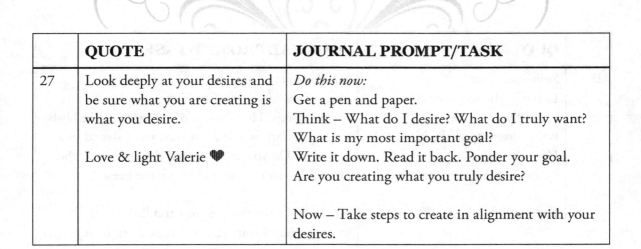

	QUOTE	JOURNAL PROMPT/TASK
27	Look deeply at your desires and be sure what you are creating is what you desire. Love & light Valerie ♥	*Do this now:* Get a pen and paper. Think – What do I desire? What do I truly want? What is my most important goal? Write it down. Read it back. Ponder your goal. Are you creating what you truly desire? Now – Take steps to create in alignment with your desires.

	QUOTE	JOURNAL PROMPT/TASK
28	Stop and listen. Listen to the sounds around you. Enjoy listening to the birds. Hear the bees. Be in the present moment. Love & light Valerie ♥	*Ask this now:* How often do you stop and listen to your surroundings? How often do you listen to the birds singing? When was the last time you listened to a bee hum? Do you ever take the time to watch the birds? Do you ever sit and watch the bees? Now – Take the time to stop and listen to the sounds around you. Take the time to stop and enjoy your surroundings.

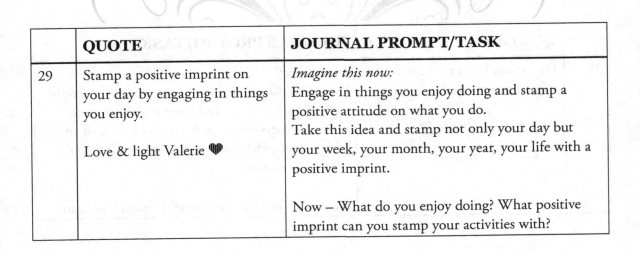

	QUOTE	JOURNAL PROMPT/TASK
29	Stamp a positive imprint on your day by engaging in things you enjoy. Love & light Valerie 🖤	*Imagine this now:* Engage in things you enjoy doing and stamp a positive attitude on what you do. Take this idea and stamp not only your day but your week, your month, your year, your life with a positive imprint. Now – What do you enjoy doing? What positive imprint can you stamp your activities with?

	QUOTE	JOURNAL PROMPT/TASK
30	Open your heart to the beauty that surrounds us. Love & light Valerie ♥	*Do the now:* Pause and place your hands over your heart – right over left. With your hands over your heart take your awareness into your heart. Look around you with that heartfelt awareness. Look around you with appreciation. Now – See your surroundings through you heart.

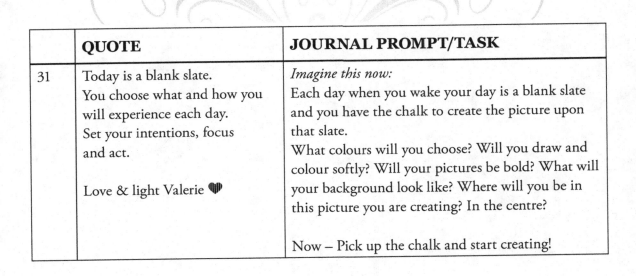

	QUOTE	JOURNAL PROMPT/TASK
31	Today is a blank slate. You choose what and how you will experience each day. Set your intentions, focus and act. Love & light Valerie	*Imagine this now:* Each day when you wake your day is a blank slate and you have the chalk to create the picture upon that slate. What colours will you choose? Will you draw and colour softly? Will your pictures be bold? What will your background look like? Where will you be in this picture you are creating? In the centre? Now – Pick up the chalk and start creating!

6. Choose Hope Over Despair

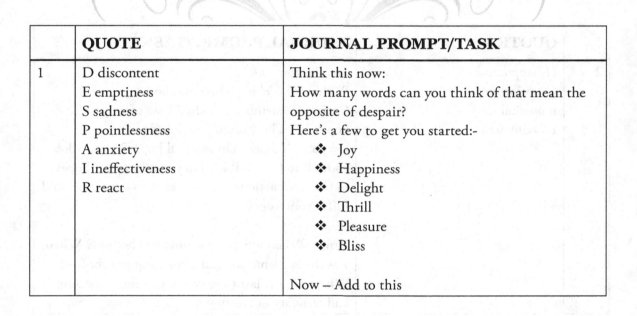

	QUOTE	JOURNAL PROMPT/TASK
1	D discontent E emptiness S sadness P pointlessness A anxiety I ineffectiveness R react	Think this now: How many words can you think of that mean the opposite of despair? Here's a few to get you started:- ❖ Joy ❖ Happiness ❖ Delight ❖ Thrill ❖ Pleasure ❖ Bliss Now – Add to this

	QUOTE	JOURNAL PROMPT/TASK
2	H happiness O optimism P possibilities E excitement	*Imagine this now:* Without the 'e' hope becomes hop. Can you remember as a child how often you hopped and how often you hoped? Do you still hope? Do you still hop? Do you allow yourself to be childlike? Do you allow your hopes to fuel your actions and thus create your desires and fulfill your hopes? Now – When was the last time you hopped? When was the last time you did something just for fun? When was the last time you hoped for something and went about creating it?

	QUOTE	JOURNAL PROMPT/TASK
3	Focus your intentions on your desires in life. See the highest possible solutions and outcomes. Love & light Valerie 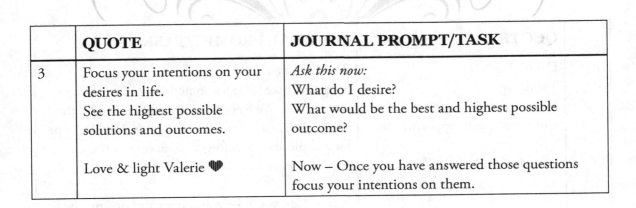	*Ask this now:* What do I desire? What would be the best and highest possible outcome? Now – Once you have answered those questions focus your intentions on them.

	QUOTE	JOURNAL PROMPT/TASK
4	Dream big. Think big. Be your own inspiration. Create your own opportunities. Love & light Valerie 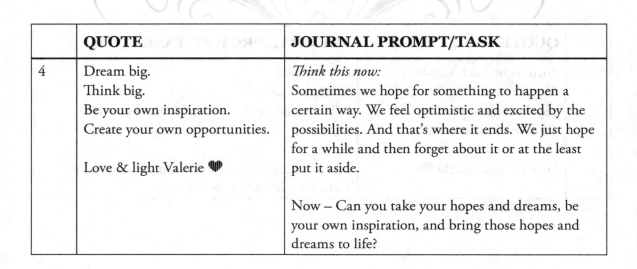	*Think this now:* Sometimes we hope for something to happen a certain way. We feel optimistic and excited by the possibilities. And that's where it ends. We just hope for a while and then forget about it or at the least put it aside. Now – Can you take your hopes and dreams, be your own inspiration, and bring those hopes and dreams to life?

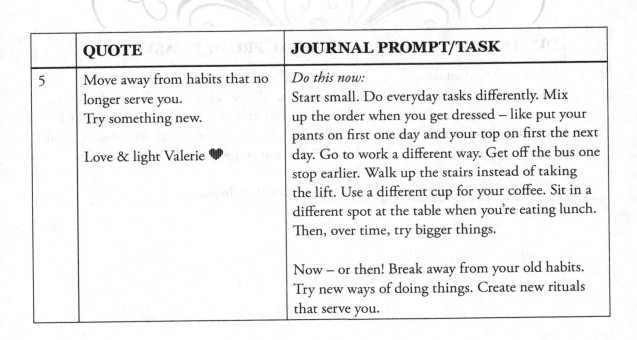

	QUOTE	JOURNAL PROMPT/TASK
5	Move away from habits that no longer serve you. Try something new. Love & light Valerie ♥	*Do this now:* Start small. Do everyday tasks differently. Mix up the order when you get dressed – like put your pants on first one day and your top on first the next day. Go to work a different way. Get off the bus one stop earlier. Walk up the stairs instead of taking the lift. Use a different cup for your coffee. Sit in a different spot at the table when you're eating lunch. Then, over time, try bigger things. Now – or then! Break away from your old habits. Try new ways of doing things. Create new rituals that serve you.

	QUOTE	JOURNAL PROMPT/TASK
6	Focus on what you desire. Imagine it already is. Love & light Valerie 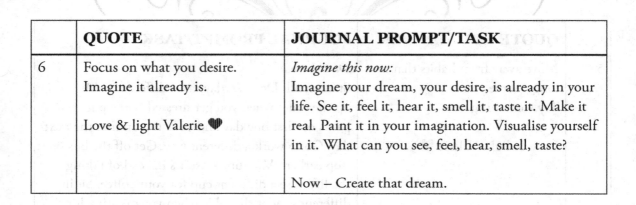	*Imagine this now:* Imagine your dream, your desire, is already in your life. See it, feel it, hear it, smell it, taste it. Make it real. Paint it in your imagination. Visualise yourself in it. What can you see, feel, hear, smell, taste? Now – Create that dream.

	QUOTE	JOURNAL PROMPT/TASK
7	Listen to your heart before making decisions. Attune to yourself. Love & light Valerie 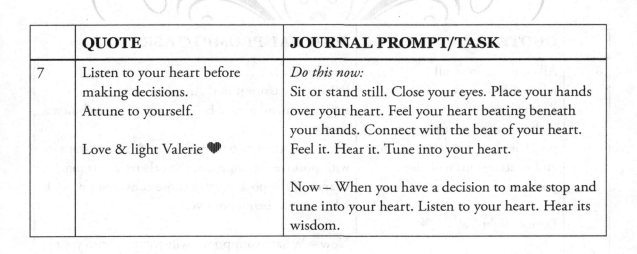	*Do this now:* Sit or stand still. Close your eyes. Place your hands over your heart. Feel your heart beating beneath your hands. Connect with the beat of your heart. Feel it. Hear it. Tune into your heart. Now – When you have a decision to make stop and tune into your heart. Listen to your heart. Hear its wisdom.

	QUOTE	JOURNAL PROMPT/TASK
8	All conversations, all relationships start with assumptions. If those assumptions start positive, then our conversations and relationships will also be positive. Love & light Valerie ♥	*Think this now:* What is an assumption? An assumption is a supposition, an idea, a belief, a guess, a possibility, a theory. If we start all our conversations and relationships with positive assumptions, then there is a strong chance of the possibility of those conversations and relationships being positive. Now – What assumptions will you take into your next conversation?

	QUOTE	JOURNAL PROMPT/TASK
9	Make it your choice to focus on the positive today. Make it your choice to focus on the positive tomorrow. Love & light Valerie 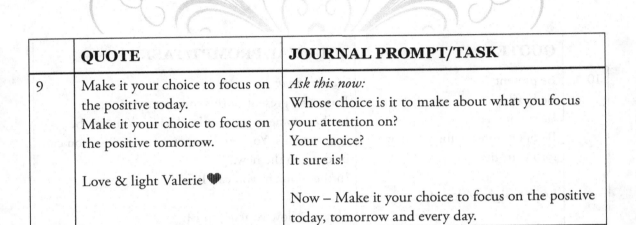	*Ask this now:* Whose choice is it to make about what you focus your attention on? Your choice? It sure is! Now – Make it your choice to focus on the positive today, tomorrow and every day.

	QUOTE	JOURNAL PROMPT/TASK
10	Be present. Be flexible. Be spontaneous. Be open to receiving the new into your life. Love & light Valerie 🖤	*Do this now:* Pause. Be present in this moment. In this moment you can be flexible. You can be spontaneous. You can be open to receiving. You can be open to the new. In the moment you can BE. Now – Allow yourself to BE.

	QUOTE	JOURNAL PROMPT/TASK
11	Set your intention before you act. Love & light Valerie 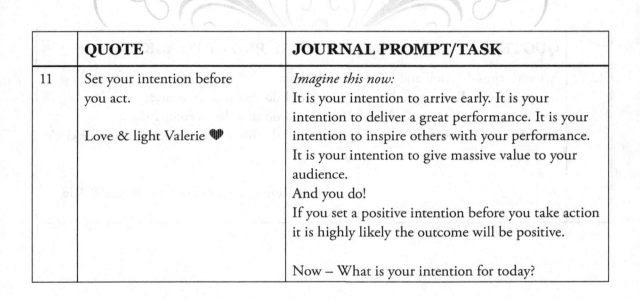	*Imagine this now:* It is your intention to arrive early. It is your intention to deliver a great performance. It is your intention to inspire others with your performance. It is your intention to give massive value to your audience. And you do! If you set a positive intention before you take action it is highly likely the outcome will be positive. Now – What is your intention for today?

	QUOTE	JOURNAL PROMPT/TASK
12	Act with consideration and compassion in all that you do. Love & light Valerie 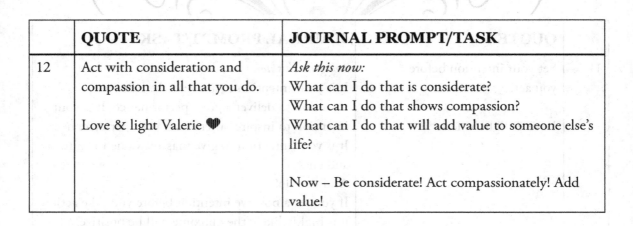	*Ask this now:* What can I do that is considerate? What can I do that shows compassion? What can I do that will add value to someone else's life? Now – Be considerate! Act compassionately! Add value!

	QUOTE	JOURNAL PROMPT/TASK
13	Everything looks brighter when seen through loving eyes. Love & light Valerie ❤	*Think this now:* Like the saying about looking at things through rose coloured glasses, when we look at anything through the eyes of love it is going to look rosier. Now – Put on your love glasses.

	QUOTE	JOURNAL PROMPT/TASK
14	Keep dreaming! Always dream. Set goals. But take action too. Love & light Valerie ❤	*Imagine this now:* Picture the life you desire being a reality. Dream it! See it! Set goals that will enable you to achieve the dream. But don't stop there. Once you set a goal you need to set steps in place to achieve it. Without goals or action your dreams will always be just that – Dreams! Now – What goal can you set? And what action can you take?

	QUOTE	JOURNAL PROMPT/TASK
15	Bring variety and pleasure into your life. Focus on fun and relaxing activities. Love & light Valerie ♥	*Do this now:* If you are not experiencing some variety or pleasure, or engaging in fun, relaxing activities – Adjust your focus. Now – Have some fun! Choose activities that bring you pleasure.

	QUOTE	JOURNAL PROMPT/TASK
16	Imagine you are living your best life today. Allow it to be. Love & light Valerie 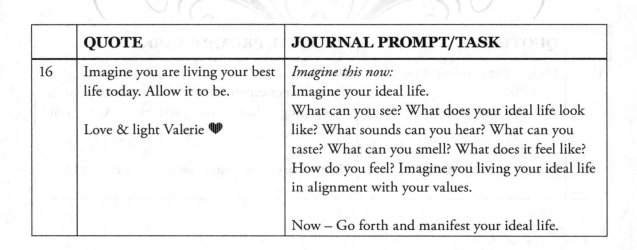	*Imagine this now:* Imagine your ideal life. What can you see? What does your ideal life look like? What sounds can you hear? What can you taste? What can you smell? What does it feel like? How do you feel? Imagine you living your ideal life in alignment with your values. Now – Go forth and manifest your ideal life.

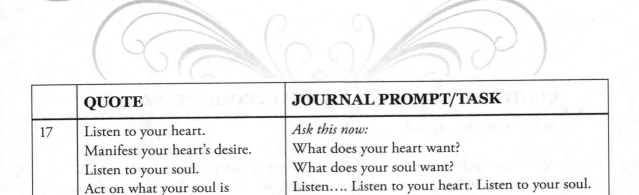

	QUOTE	JOURNAL PROMPT/TASK
17	Listen to your heart. Manifest your heart's desire. Listen to your soul. Act on what your soul is telling you. Love & light Valerie ♥	*Ask this now:* What does your heart want? What does your soul want? Listen…. Listen to your heart. Listen to your soul. Now – Act on what you hear. Act on what your heart and soul are telling you.

	QUOTE	JOURNAL PROMPT/TASK
18	Focus on love, beauty and balance. Inject these qualities into everything you do. Seek harmony within and project it out. Love & light Valerie ♥	*Do this now:* Centre yourself. Place your hands over your heart and close your eyes. Breath in and out slowly while focusing on your Heart – Your Centre – Your Soul. See the beauty within you. Feel the beauty within you. Focus on the beauty within you. Focus on love. Focus on everything being balanced as you breathe in and out. Seek your inner harmony. Inject love, beauty and balance into everything you do. Project your inner harmony outwards. Now – Adjust your focus so that what you are seeing in everything you look at is centred on love, beauty and balance, and share that love, beauty and harmony.

	QUOTE	JOURNAL PROMPT/TASK
19	Be still. Be silent. Be present. Be love. Love & light Valerie 🖤	*Think this now:* Do I have to DO to BE? The best answer to that question is no! When we are constantly busy and doing things, we are not allowing ourselves to be. Are you a human DOing or a human BEing? Now – BE!

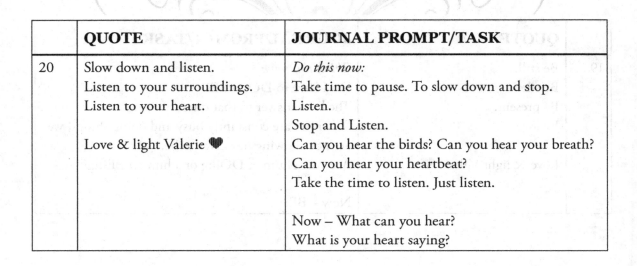

	QUOTE	JOURNAL PROMPT/TASK
20	Slow down and listen. Listen to your surroundings. Listen to your heart. Love & light Valerie 🖤	*Do this now:* Take time to pause. To slow down and stop. Listen. Stop and Listen. Can you hear the birds? Can you hear your breath? Can you hear your heartbeat? Take the time to listen. Just listen. Now – What can you hear? What is your heart saying?

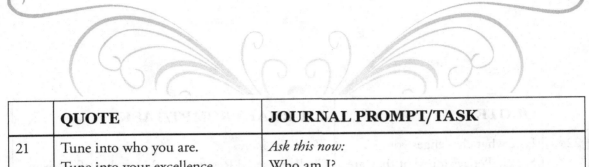

	QUOTE	JOURNAL PROMPT/TASK
21	Tune into who you are. Tune into your excellence. Value who you are and your excellence. Love & light Valerie 🖤	*Ask this now:* Who am I? What am I good at? What are my gifts and talents? What challenges have I overcome? When you value who you are and your excellence – Your gifts and talents – What you are good at – You are able to value others, and they will see your value. Now – What value can you offer others?

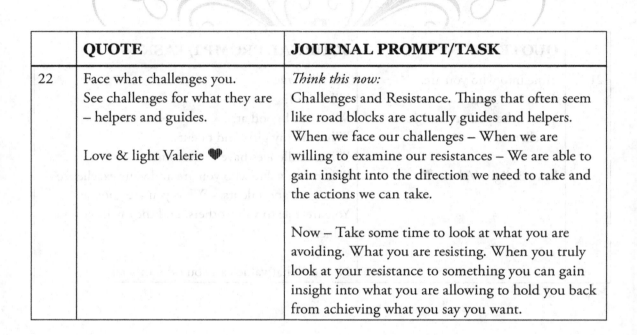

	QUOTE	JOURNAL PROMPT/TASK
22	Face what challenges you. See challenges for what they are – helpers and guides. Love & light Valerie ♥	*Think this now:* Challenges and Resistance. Things that often seem like road blocks are actually guides and helpers. When we face our challenges – When we are willing to examine our resistances – We are able to gain insight into the direction we need to take and the actions we can take. Now – Take some time to look at what you are avoiding. What you are resisting. When you truly look at your resistance to something you can gain insight into what you are allowing to hold you back from achieving what you say you want.

	QUOTE	JOURNAL PROMPT/TASK
23	Speak and act from the heart. The world changes because of people who speak out. Be part of the change. Love & light Valerie 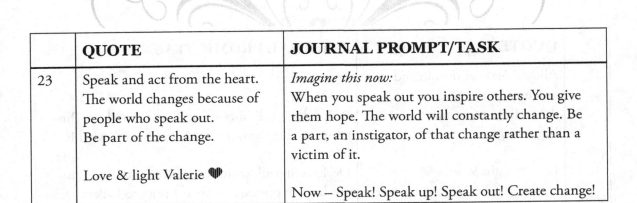	*Imagine this now:* When you speak out you inspire others. You give them hope. The world will constantly change. Be a part, an instigator, of that change rather than a victim of it. Now – Speak! Speak up! Speak out! Create change!

	QUOTE	JOURNAL PROMPT/TASK
24	Allow release of the old and thus welcome in the new. All endings mean new beginnings. Love & light Valerie 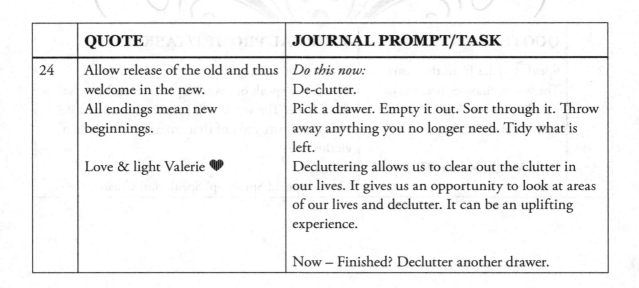	*Do this now:* De-clutter. Pick a drawer. Empty it out. Sort through it. Throw away anything you no longer need. Tidy what is left. Decluttering allows us to clear out the clutter in our lives. It gives us an opportunity to look at areas of our lives and declutter. It can be an uplifting experience. Now – Finished? Declutter another drawer.

	QUOTE	JOURNAL PROMPT/TASK
25	Drop any falsehood, and simply be who you are. Be the genuine, authentic you! Love & light Valerie 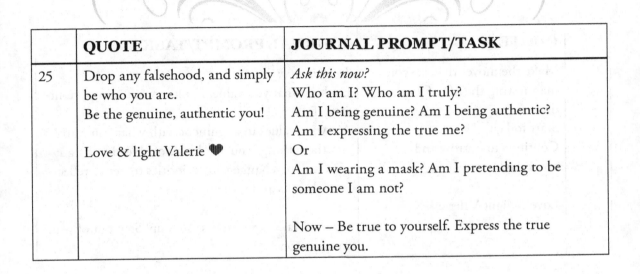	*Ask this now?* Who am I? Who am I truly? Am I being genuine? Am I being authentic? Am I expressing the true me? Or Am I wearing a mask? Am I pretending to be someone I am not? Now – Be true to yourself. Express the true genuine you.

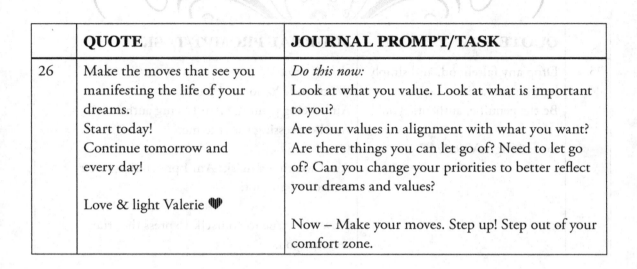

	QUOTE	JOURNAL PROMPT/TASK
26	Make the moves that see you manifesting the life of your dreams. Start today! Continue tomorrow and every day! Love & light Valerie ❤	*Do this now:* Look at what you value. Look at what is important to you? Are your values in alignment with what you want? Are there things you can let go of? Need to let go of? Can you change your priorities to better reflect your dreams and values? Now – Make your moves. Step up! Step out of your comfort zone.

	QUOTE	JOURNAL PROMPT/TASK
27	Let go of concerns. Let go of worries. Naturally release. Observe what happens next. Love & light Valerie 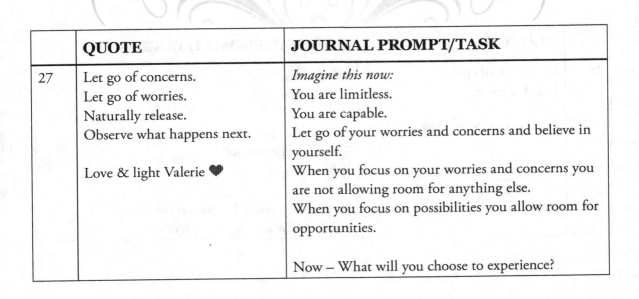	*Imagine this now:* You are limitless. You are capable. Let go of your worries and concerns and believe in yourself. When you focus on your worries and concerns you are not allowing room for anything else. When you focus on possibilities you allow room for opportunities. Now – What will you choose to experience?

	QUOTE	JOURNAL PROMPT/TASK
28	Give yourself credit. You deserve it. Love & light Valerie 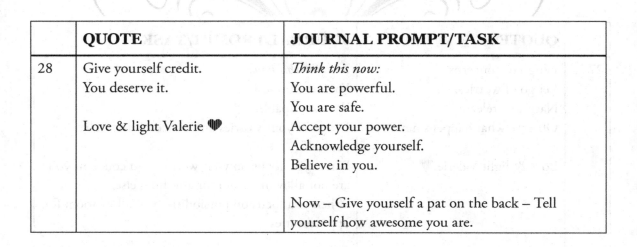	*Think this now:* You are powerful. You are safe. Accept your power. Acknowledge yourself. Believe in you. Now – Give yourself a pat on the back – Tell yourself how awesome you are.

	QUOTE	JOURNAL PROMPT/TASK
29	You set the tone for each day. What tone do you wish to live today? It's your choice. Love & light Valerie 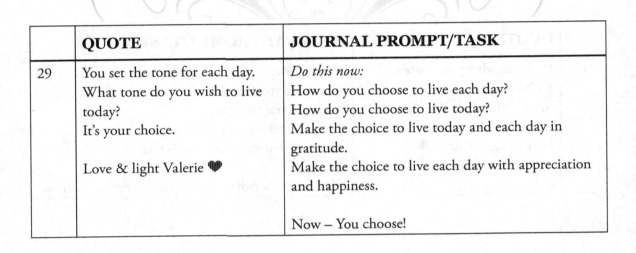	*Do this now:* How do you choose to live each day? How do you choose to live today? Make the choice to live today and each day in gratitude. Make the choice to live each day with appreciation and happiness. Now – You choose!

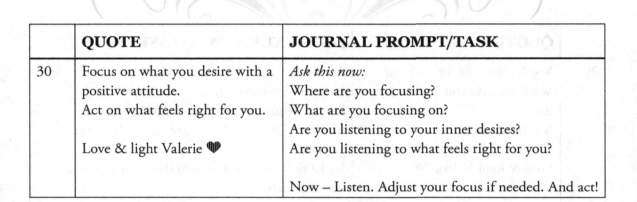

	QUOTE	JOURNAL PROMPT/TASK
30	Focus on what you desire with a positive attitude. Act on what feels right for you. Love & light Valerie 🖤	*Ask this now:* Where are you focusing? What are you focusing on? Are you listening to your inner desires? Are you listening to what feels right for you? Now – Listen. Adjust your focus if needed. And act!

7. Choose Focus Over Distraction

	QUOTE	JOURNAL PROMPT/TASK
1	D disruption I interruption S stop T target R response A attention T trigger I interest O other options N notice	*Think this now:* You are working on a project. You have a deadline to meet, and you're going well. You will get it done on time. Then your phone beeps and you glace to see what is coming in. It's a message from a friend. You know you should stay focused, but you decide to just read it. You read it. Then you decide to just reply. It won't take long. Your friend then replies, and you stop to reply once again. And again, and again. Now you haven't finished the project and it is due in 5 minutes! Now – Can you relate to this? I think most people can. Next time you are tempted to be distracted consider your behaviour. Consider the consequences of your actions.

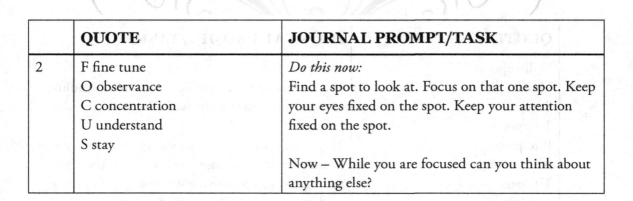

	QUOTE	JOURNAL PROMPT/TASK
2	F fine tune O observance C concentration U understand S stay	*Do this now:* Find a spot to look at. Focus on that one spot. Keep your eyes fixed on the spot. Keep your attention fixed on the spot. Now – While you are focused can you think about anything else?

	QUOTE	JOURNAL PROMPT/TASK
3	Slow down and focus on one thing at a time. Ground yourself in each moment. Love & light Valerie 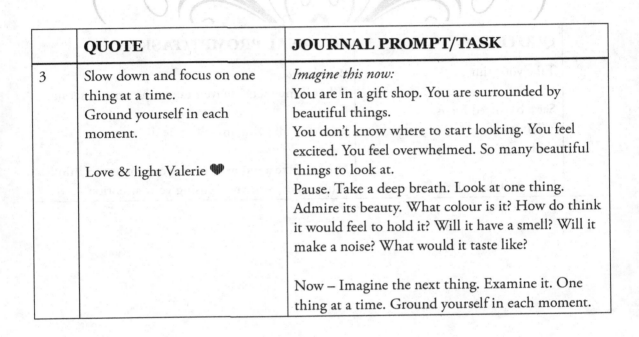	*Imagine this now:* You are in a gift shop. You are surrounded by beautiful things. You don't know where to start looking. You feel excited. You feel overwhelmed. So many beautiful things to look at. Pause. Take a deep breath. Look at one thing. Admire its beauty. What colour is it? How do think it would feel to hold it? Will it have a smell? Will it make a noise? What would it taste like? Now – Imagine the next thing. Examine it. One thing at a time. Ground yourself in each moment.

	QUOTE	JOURNAL PROMPT/TASK
4	Take your time. Set your focus. Set a balanced focus. What you focus on is your choice. Love & light Valerie 🖤	*Ask this now:* What is my focus? Have I taken the time to set my focus? Or. Am I allowing myself to be distracted? Now – Take a moment to set your focus. To think about where you are focusing your attention.

	QUOTE	JOURNAL PROMPT/TASK
5	Focus on the positives in your life. Focus on your abilities and talents. And manifest! Love & light Valerie ♥	*Think this now:* We all have abilities and talents. Do you acknowledge your abilities and talents? Do you focus on them and use then to enhance your life? Do you acknowledge the things in your life you can be grateful for? Do you focus on them? Now – Focus on the positives – Focus on your gifts and talents – Share them with the world.

	QUOTE	JOURNAL PROMPT/TASK
6	Be wise. Be mature. Ask yourself... How can I improve my responses to situations in my life? Love & light Valerie 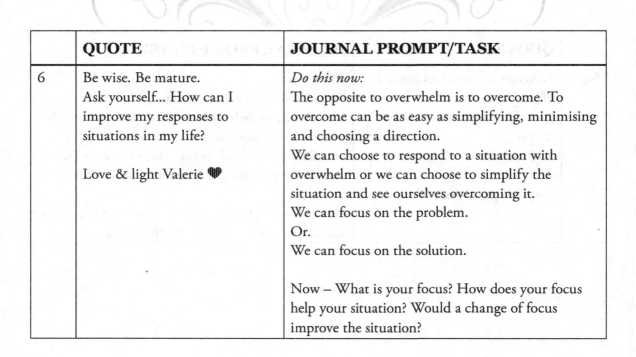	*Do this now:* The opposite to overwhelm is to overcome. To overcome can be as easy as simplifying, minimising and choosing a direction. We can choose to respond to a situation with overwhelm or we can choose to simplify the situation and see ourselves overcoming it. We can focus on the problem. Or. We can focus on the solution. Now – What is your focus? How does your focus help your situation? Would a change of focus improve the situation?

	QUOTE	JOURNAL PROMPT/TASK
7	Focus on the uniqueness you bring to the world. Love & light Valerie 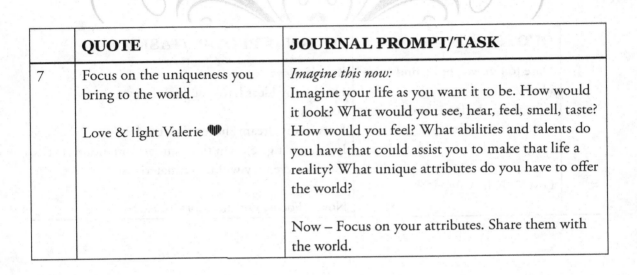	*Imagine this now:* Imagine your life as you want it to be. How would it look? What would you see, hear, feel, smell, taste? How would you feel? What abilities and talents do you have that could assist you to make that life a reality? What unique attributes do you have to offer the world? Now – Focus on your attributes. Share them with the world.

	QUOTE	JOURNAL PROMPT/TASK
8	Dare to put weight behind your ideas. Give them the focus and attention they deserve. Forge ahead. Love & light Valerie ❤	*Ask this now:* How many ideas have you had that you haven't acted on? How many dreams have you let fade? If you don't give them the focus and attention that they deserve they will never materialise. Now – Focus. Put the effort in. Act!

	QUOTE	JOURNAL PROMPT/TASK
9	Focus on Being: Being grounded. Being adventurous. Being inspired, Being all that you can be. Being you. And let you, Be enough! Love & light Valerie 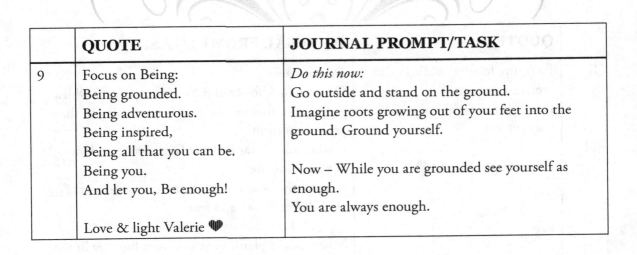	*Do this now:* Go outside and stand on the ground. Imagine roots growing out of your feet into the ground. Ground yourself. Now – While you are grounded see yourself as enough. You are always enough.

	QUOTE	JOURNAL PROMPT/TASK
10	Be future focused while in the present moment. Don't go too far ahead or you may get lost. Love & light Valerie ♥	*Do this now:* Can you look forward to your future plans whilst you remain focused on what is happening in the present moment? If you look too far into the future you can lose sight of where you are. Constantly focusing ahead can cause feelings of overwhelm, worry and fear. Now – Make plans for your future but stay in the present moment and take present moment actions.

	QUOTE	JOURNAL PROMPT/TASK
11	Where are you focussing your attention? What is your intention? It's your choice. Love & light Valerie 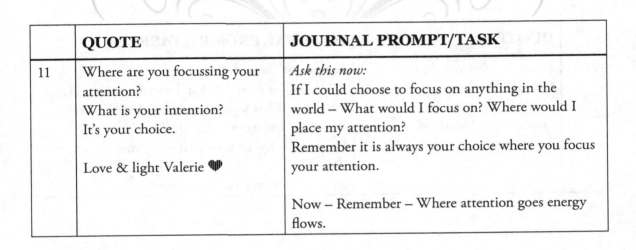	*Ask this now:* If I could choose to focus on anything in the world – What would I focus on? Where would I place my attention? Remember it is always your choice where you focus your attention. Now – Remember – Where attention goes energy flows.

	QUOTE	JOURNAL PROMPT/TASK
12	Focus on what you desire. Strengthen your resolve. Love & light Valerie 🖤	*Imagine this now:* What do you desire? What does your dream life look like? What legacy would you like to leave? Focus on that. Focus on your 'Why'. Let your 'Why' be your purpose – your drive. Now – Be strong. Be determined.

	QUOTE	JOURNAL PROMPT/TASK
13	Rather than lamenting over what is out of your control, focus on what is yours to own, and apply yourself to what is right in front of you. Love & light Valerie ♥	*Think this now:* Is the weather within your control? Is someone else's behaviour within your control? We can only control our own behaviour. And our behaviour is dependent on our thoughts and how we respond to what we are experiencing. What you choose to focus on will be different from the person standing next to you. Now – Apply yourself to your response. Own your response. Take responsibility for how you respond and let others take responsibility for how they respond.

	QUOTE	JOURNAL PROMPT/TASK
14	Choose your focus. Move through your day with focused awareness. Set a theme for your day. Love & light Valerie 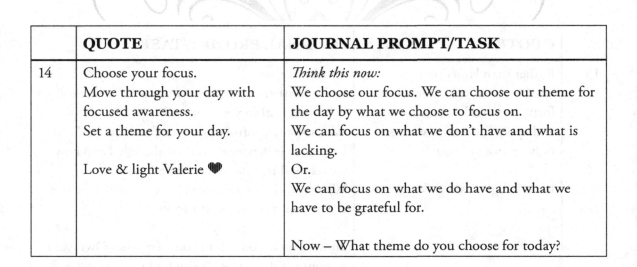	*Think this now:* We choose our focus. We can choose our theme for the day by what we choose to focus on. We can focus on what we don't have and what is lacking. Or. We can focus on what we do have and what we have to be grateful for. Now – What theme do you choose for today?

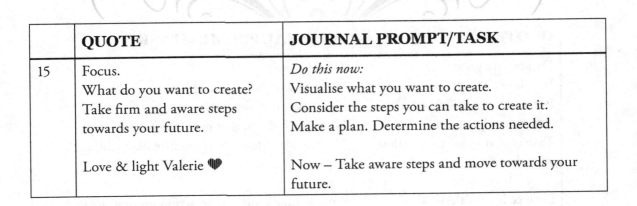

	QUOTE	JOURNAL PROMPT/TASK
15	Focus. What do you want to create? Take firm and aware steps towards your future. Love & light Valerie ♥	*Do this now:* Visualise what you want to create. Consider the steps you can take to create it. Make a plan. Determine the actions needed. Now – Take aware steps and move towards your future.

	QUOTE	JOURNAL PROMPT/TASK
16	Dreams are great. We all need to dream. But without action they will always just be dreams. Take action today to manifest your dreams. Love & light Valerie ♥	*Do this now:* Write down one of your dreams. Now reword it as a goal. Now break down that goal into smaller steps. Now break it down into even smaller achievable steps. Now – Take a step. Take action on that dream.

	QUOTE	JOURNAL PROMPT/TASK
17	Focus on one thing at a time. And do that with love for yourself. And allow that love to flow on to others. Love & light Valerie ♥	*Imagine this now:* You are trying to focus on creating something – an artwork, a meal, or a work project while feeling angry. How do you think your creation will turn out? Now – Whatever your focus, you need to back it with love; love for yourself, love for what you are doing and love for others.

	QUOTE	JOURNAL PROMPT/TASK
18	Pause and refocus. Reset. Take action. Take a step. Small or large. Just act. Love & light Valerie 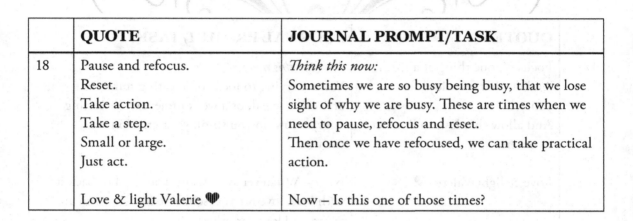	*Think this now:* Sometimes we are so busy being busy, that we lose sight of why we are busy. These are times when we need to pause, refocus and reset. Then once we have refocused, we can take practical action. Now – Is this one of those times?

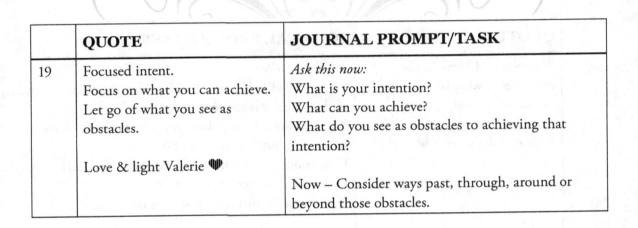

	QUOTE	JOURNAL PROMPT/TASK
19	Focused intent. Focus on what you can achieve. Let go of what you see as obstacles. Love & light Valerie 💗	*Ask this now:* What is your intention? What can you achieve? What do you see as obstacles to achieving that intention? Now – Consider ways past, through, around or beyond those obstacles.

	QUOTE	JOURNAL PROMPT/TASK
20	Focus on and move in the direction of what is most important to you. Love & light Valerie ♥	*Imagine this now:* You are heading off on a holiday. Your bags are packed. You're ready to leave. But. You don't know where you are going. You have no destination. You have no direction. If you don't know where you are going you don't know which direction to move in. If you have no direction you have no focus. Now –Determine your 'Why' – Then you will know what direction to take and where to focus your energy.

	QUOTE	JOURNAL PROMPT/TASK
21	Pause. Consider. Assess. Love & light Valerie 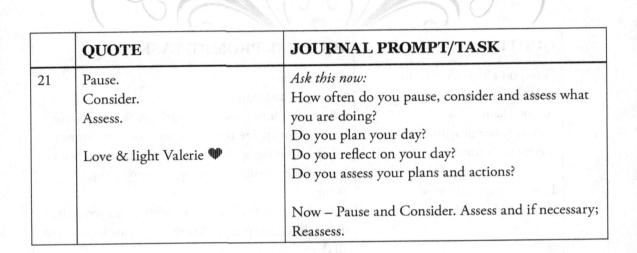	*Ask this now:* How often do you pause, consider and assess what you are doing? Do you plan your day? Do you reflect on your day? Do you assess your plans and actions? Now – Pause and Consider. Assess and if necessary; Reassess.

	QUOTE	JOURNAL PROMPT/TASK
22	Focus on allowing your inner visions to rise to the surface. Act on them. Follow through with tenacity. Create your dreams. Love & light Valerie 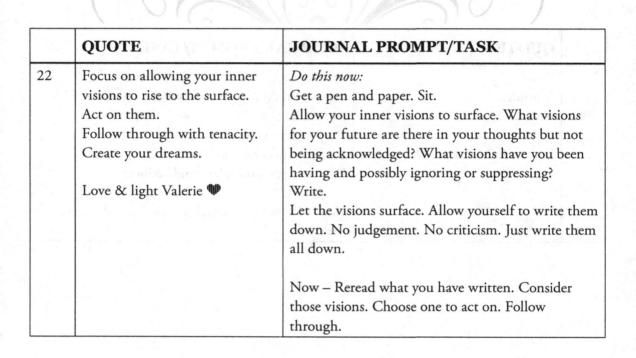	*Do this now:* Get a pen and paper. Sit. Allow your inner visions to surface. What visions for your future are there in your thoughts but not being acknowledged? What visions have you been having and possibly ignoring or suppressing? Write. Let the visions surface. Allow yourself to write them down. No judgement. No criticism. Just write them all down. Now – Reread what you have written. Consider those visions. Choose one to act on. Follow through.

	QUOTE	JOURNAL PROMPT/TASK
23	Take a moment to be in the moment. Don't rush. Take it a little slower. Pause and appreciate your surroundings. Love & light Valerie ♥	*Think this now:* When we rush to get here and get there – to fit everything in we become fixated. We only see immediately in front of us. If you choose to take it a little slower, you can see and appreciate much more. Now – What can you see? What is right in front of you? What can you see if you look around?

	QUOTE	JOURNAL PROMPT/TASK
24	Remember the law of attraction. What we focus on is what we attract. Focus on lack and limitation – and you will attract more lack and limitation. Focus on abundance – and you will attract more abundance. Love & light Valerie ♥	*Imagine this now:* How often have you been thinking of someone and then they ring you or you meet them at the supermarket? Is it chance? Is it coincidence? Is it fate? It has been said that all our thoughts turn into something eventually. Now – Think intentionally. Focus on what you would like to attract into your life, rather than what you wouldn't like.

	QUOTE	JOURNAL PROMPT/TASK
25	Respond to what needs your attention. Identify what needs to change and make changes. Have a purpose. Commit to your purpose. Let go of worry about the outcome. Trust. Love & light Valerie ♥	*Do this now:* Consider what you need to prioritise today? What needs your attention? What do you need to focus on? Identify if you need to make any changes. What needs to change? Have a purpose for what you do – what you prioritise – what you focus on. Commit to that purpose. Now – Trust.

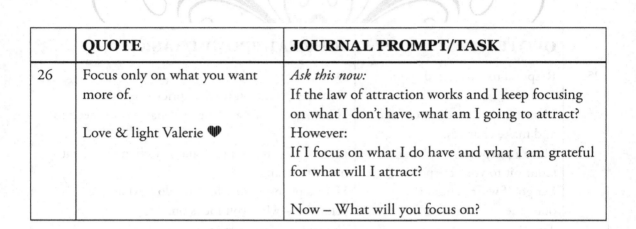

	QUOTE	JOURNAL PROMPT/TASK
26	Focus only on what you want more of. Love & light Valerie 🖤	*Ask this now:* If the law of attraction works and I keep focusing on what I don't have, what am I going to attract? However: If I focus on what I do have and what I am grateful for what will I attract? Now – What will you focus on?

	QUOTE	JOURNAL PROMPT/TASK
27	Focus on self-care. Enjoy your own company. Be a centre of calm. Love & light Valerie 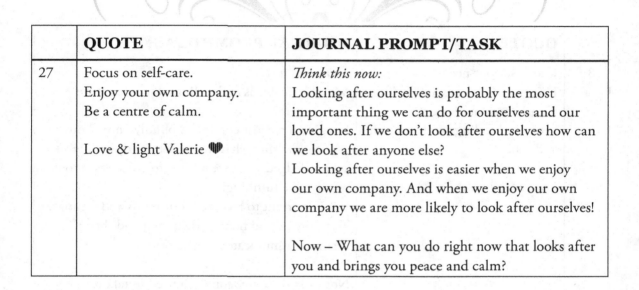	*Think this now:* Looking after ourselves is probably the most important thing we can do for ourselves and our loved ones. If we don't look after ourselves how can we look after anyone else? Looking after ourselves is easier when we enjoy our own company. And when we enjoy our own company we are more likely to look after ourselves! Now – What can you do right now that looks after you and brings you peace and calm?

	QUOTE	JOURNAL PROMPT/TASK
28	Prioritise your needs. Honour your needs and feelings. Clearly communicate your needs and feelings with yourself and others. Love & light Valerie 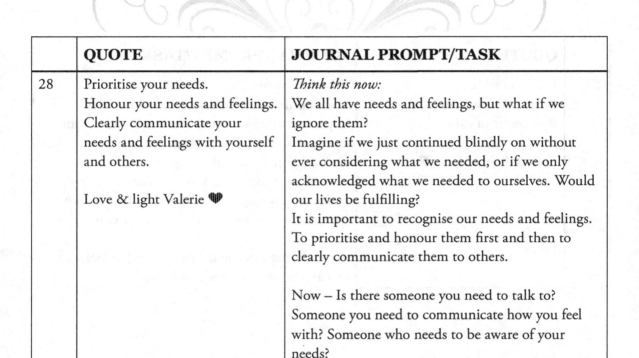	*Think this now:* We all have needs and feelings, but what if we ignore them? Imagine if we just continued blindly on without ever considering what we needed, or if we only acknowledged what we needed to ourselves. Would our lives be fulfilling? It is important to recognise our needs and feelings. To prioritise and honour them first and then to clearly communicate them to others. Now – Is there someone you need to talk to? Someone you need to communicate how you feel with? Someone who needs to be aware of your needs?

	QUOTE	JOURNAL PROMPT/TASK
29	Focus on what interests you the most. Love & light Valerie ♥	*Ask this now:* What do you love doing? What would you do just for the sheer pleasure of doing it? What is that you can totally lose track of time doing? What brings a smile to your face just thinking about it? Now – Focus on it. Even if only for a short while – Focus on it.

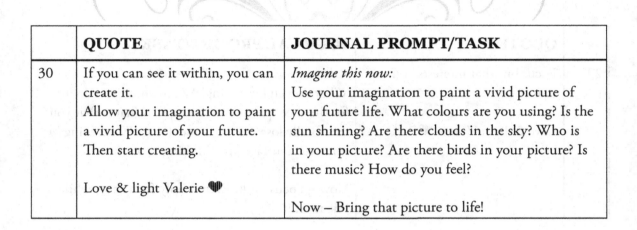

	QUOTE	JOURNAL PROMPT/TASK
30	If you can see it within, you can create it. Allow your imagination to paint a vivid picture of your future. Then start creating. Love & light Valerie 🖤	*Imagine this now:* Use your imagination to paint a vivid picture of your future life. What colours are you using? Is the sun shining? Are there clouds in the sky? Who is in your picture? Are there birds in your picture? Is there music? How do you feel? Now – Bring that picture to life!

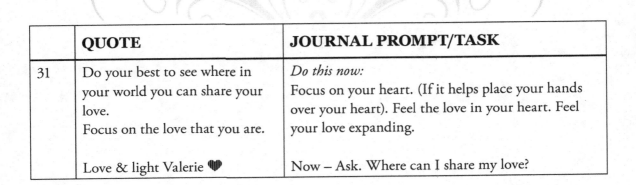

	QUOTE	JOURNAL PROMPT/TASK
31	Do your best to see where in your world you can share your love. Focus on the love that you are. Love & light Valerie ♥	*Do this now:* Focus on your heart. (If it helps place your hands over your heart). Feel the love in your heart. Feel your love expanding. Now – Ask. Where can I share my love?

8. Choose Less Over More

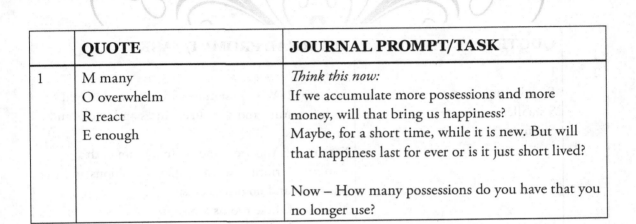

	QUOTE	JOURNAL PROMPT/TASK
1	M many O overwhelm R react E enough	*Think this now:* If we accumulate more possessions and more money, will that bring us happiness? Maybe, for a short time, while it is new. But will that happiness last for ever or is it just short lived? Now – How many possessions do you have that you no longer use?

	QUOTE	JOURNAL PROMPT/TASK
2	L lower E excluding S smaller S simple	*Imagine this now:* Scenario 1: You are standing in a room cluttered with furniture and soft furnishings and books and ornaments. Scenario 2: You are standing in a room with minimal furniture and a couple of cushions and a one book and no ornaments. Neither of these rooms are yours. You have been asked to clean these rooms thoroughly. Now – Which one would you prefer to clean?

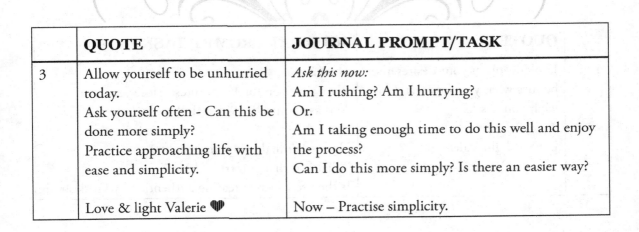

	QUOTE	JOURNAL PROMPT/TASK
3	Allow yourself to be unhurried today. Ask yourself often - Can this be done more simply? Practice approaching life with ease and simplicity. Love & light Valerie	*Ask this now:* Am I rushing? Am I hurrying? Or. Am I taking enough time to do this well and enjoy the process? Can I do this more simply? Is there an easier way? Now – Practise simplicity.

	QUOTE	JOURNAL PROMPT/TASK
4	Look deeply at your desires and be sure what you are creating is what you desire. Love & light Valerie 	*Do this now:* Put a timer on for 15 minutes. Close your eyes. And ask yourself, "What do I truly desire?" Now – Write down your insights? What is it that you truly desire? Is the life you are creating authentic to your desires?

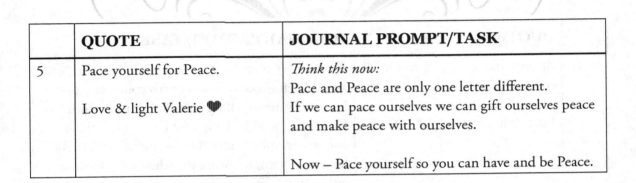

	QUOTE	JOURNAL PROMPT/TASK
5	Pace yourself for Peace. Love & light Valerie 🖤	*Think this now:* Pace and Peace are only one letter different. If we can pace ourselves we can gift ourselves peace and make peace with ourselves. Now – Pace yourself so you can have and be Peace.

	QUOTE	JOURNAL PROMPT/TASK
6	Be open, honest and direct in all conversations. Love & light Valerie ♥	*Imagine this now:* You're having a conversation with your boss. You know they aren't telling you the complete truth. Do you respond by lying too? Do you call them out on their dishonesty? Or do you be completely honest yourself, knowing that their lie will come out in time? Now – Think about how you respond when you know you are being deceived.

	QUOTE	JOURNAL PROMPT/TASK
7	Do what you can moment to moment. Every little step adds up. Let yourself see the bigger picture. Love & light Valerie ♥	*Do this now:* Sometimes when we have a dream or a goal we see only the big picture. We don't break it down. We keep looking at the dream, but it seems to be out of reach and we never take a step. We overwhelm ourselves with how impossible it seems. Yet. If we can break our dream down into smaller chunks it can become possible. So, let yourself see the bigger picture but look also at the smaller chunks and take moment to moment steps. Now –Get a pen and paper and choose a goal. Write it at the top of the page. Then break it down into smaller goals, and smaller again. Take a small step in the direction of your big dream.

	QUOTE	JOURNAL PROMPT/TASK
8	Look for creative solutions and they will appear. Love & light Valerie 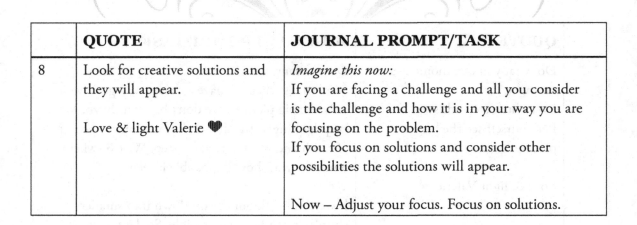	*Imagine this now:* If you are facing a challenge and all you consider is the challenge and how it is in your way you are focusing on the problem. If you focus on solutions and consider other possibilities the solutions will appear. Now – Adjust your focus. Focus on solutions.

	QUOTE	JOURNAL PROMPT/TASK
9	Trust in your visions. Act with discipline. Be thorough. Love & light Valerie 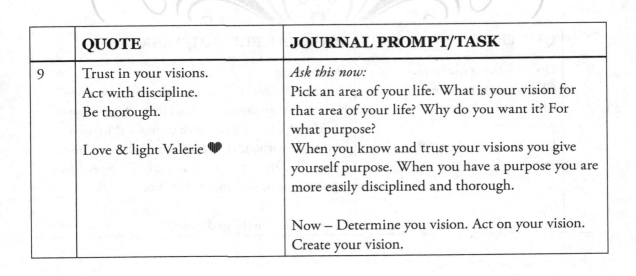	*Ask this now:* Pick an area of your life. What is your vision for that area of your life? Why do you want it? For what purpose? When you know and trust your visions you give yourself purpose. When you have a purpose you are more easily disciplined and thorough. Now – Determine you vision. Act on your vision. Create your vision.

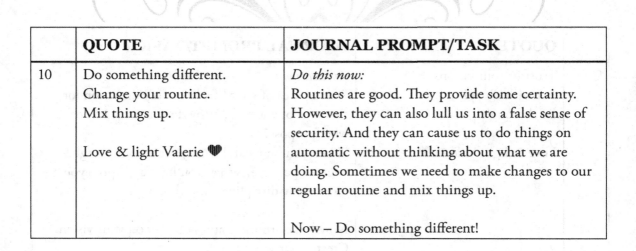

	QUOTE	JOURNAL PROMPT/TASK
10	Do something different. Change your routine. Mix things up. Love & light Valerie ♥	*Do this now:* Routines are good. They provide some certainty. However, they can also lull us into a false sense of security. And they can cause us to do things on automatic without thinking about what we are doing. Sometimes we need to make changes to our regular routine and mix things up. Now – Do something different!

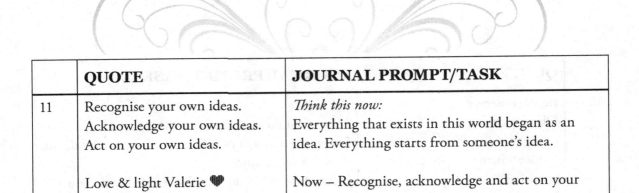

	QUOTE	JOURNAL PROMPT/TASK
11	Recognise your own ideas. Acknowledge your own ideas. Act on your own ideas. Love & light Valerie ♥	*Think this now:* Everything that exists in this world began as an idea. Everything starts from someone's idea. Now – Recognise, acknowledge and act on your ideas.

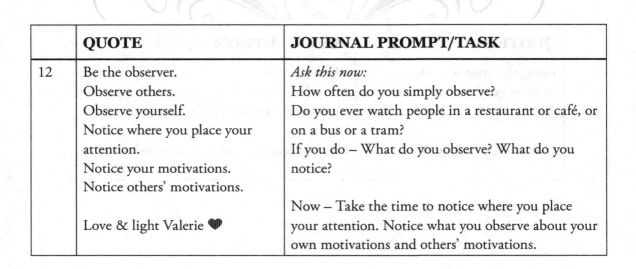

	QUOTE	JOURNAL PROMPT/TASK
12	Be the observer. Observe others. Observe yourself. Notice where you place your attention. Notice your motivations. Notice others' motivations. Love & light Valerie ♥	*Ask this now:* How often do you simply observe? Do you ever watch people in a restaurant or café, or on a bus or a tram? If you do – What do you observe? What do you notice? Now – Take the time to notice where you place your attention. Notice what you observe about your own motivations and others' motivations.

	QUOTE	JOURNAL PROMPT/TASK
11	Honour your needs. Take care of your body. And in turn your body will take care of you. Love & light Valerie 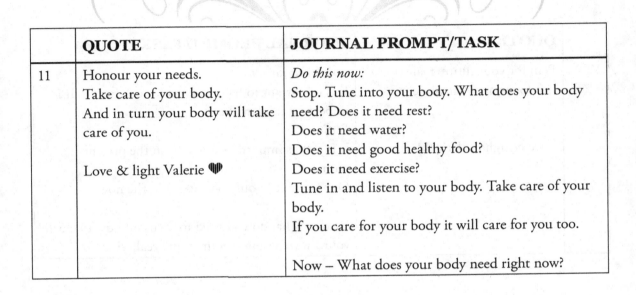	*Do this now:* Stop. Tune into your body. What does your body need? Does it need rest? Does it need water? Does it need good healthy food? Does it need exercise? Tune in and listen to your body. Take care of your body. If you care for your body it will care for you too. Now – What does your body need right now?

	QUOTE	JOURNAL PROMPT/TASK
12	Plan for your future reality. But focus on what you can do now. Love & light Valerie 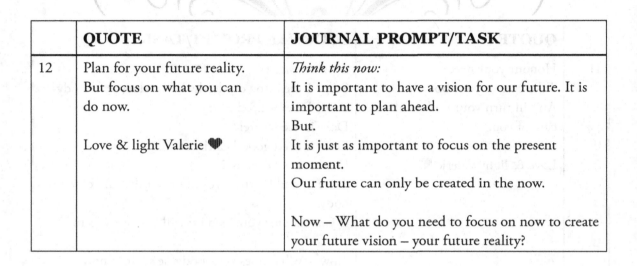	*Think this now:* It is important to have a vision for our future. It is important to plan ahead. But. It is just as important to focus on the present moment. Our future can only be created in the now. Now – What do you need to focus on now to create your future vision – your future reality?

	QUOTE	JOURNAL PROMPT/TASK
13	Take your time. Enjoy the process. Be fully immersed in each moment. Love & light Valerie 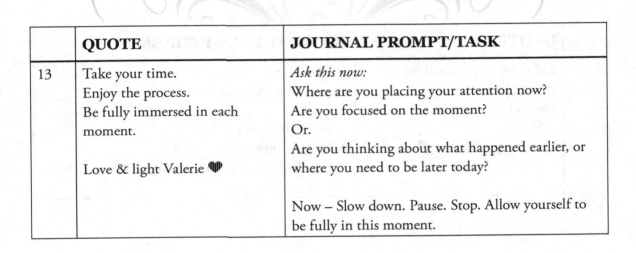	*Ask this now:* Where are you placing your attention now? Are you focused on the moment? Or. Are you thinking about what happened earlier, or where you need to be later today? Now – Slow down. Pause. Stop. Allow yourself to be fully in this moment.

	QUOTE	JOURNAL PROMPT/TASK
14	Take a break from talking. Instead listen. You can learn much. Love & light Valerie 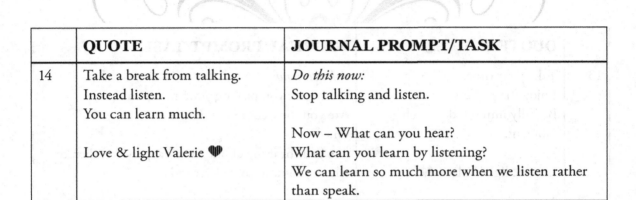	*Do this now:* Stop talking and listen. Now – What can you hear? What can you learn by listening? We can learn so much more when we listen rather than speak.

	QUOTE	JOURNAL PROMPT/TASK
16	Are you waiting for the right time to take action? Now is the right time. Don't doubt. Don't question. Now is the time to take action. Love & light Valerie 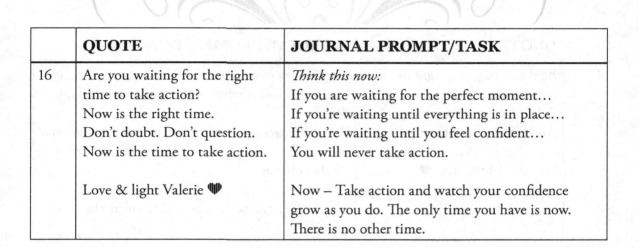	*Think this now:* If you are waiting for the perfect moment… If you're waiting until everything is in place… If you're waiting until you feel confident… You will never take action. Now – Take action and watch your confidence grow as you do. The only time you have is now. There is no other time.

	QUOTE	JOURNAL PROMPT/TASK
17	Be the change you want to see in your life. Take positive actions today. And then again tomorrow. Love & light Valerie 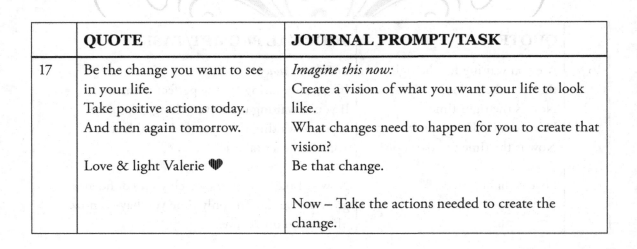	*Imagine this now:* Create a vision of what you want your life to look like. What changes need to happen for you to create that vision? Be that change. Now – Take the actions needed to create the change.

	QUOTE	JOURNAL PROMPT/TASK
18	Be personally responsible. Set and respect your own standards and boundaries. Love & light Valerie 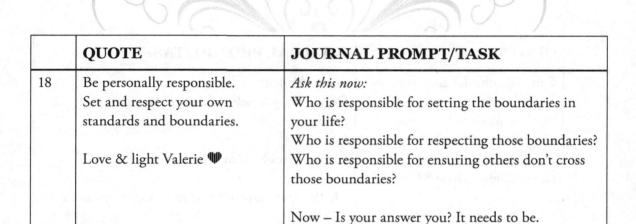	*Ask this now:* Who is responsible for setting the boundaries in your life? Who is responsible for respecting those boundaries? Who is responsible for ensuring others don't cross those boundaries? Now – Is your answer you? It needs to be.

	QUOTE	JOURNAL PROMPT/TASK
19	Can you consider challenges as opportunities? Opportunities to know your own value and worth? Love & light Valerie 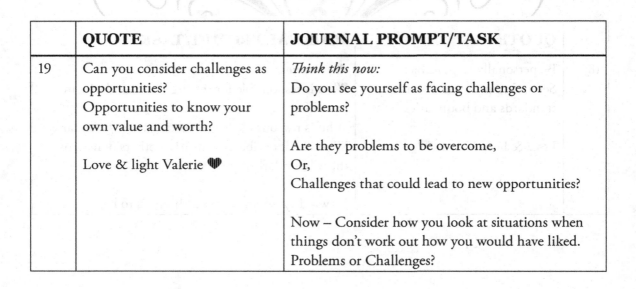	*Think this now:* Do you see yourself as facing challenges or problems? Are they problems to be overcome, Or, Challenges that could lead to new opportunities? Now – Consider how you look at situations when things don't work out how you would have liked. Problems or Challenges?

	QUOTE	JOURNAL PROMPT/TASK
20	Embrace you. Embrace life. Love & light Valerie 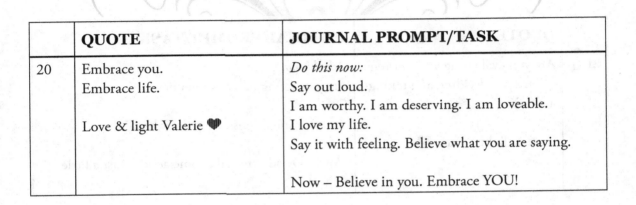	*Do this now:* Say out loud. I am worthy. I am deserving. I am loveable. I love my life. Say it with feeling. Believe what you are saying. Now – Believe in you. Embrace YOU!

	QUOTE	JOURNAL PROMPT/TASK
21	Are you evaluating and musing? Or are you deciding and taking action? Love & light Valerie 🖤	*Ask this now:* Are you acting on your intentions? Or Are your intentions just in your head? Now – Decide and take some action. Just a little step.

	QUOTE	JOURNAL PROMPT/TASK
22	Life is fluid. As you are. Allow yourself to flow. Love & light Valerie 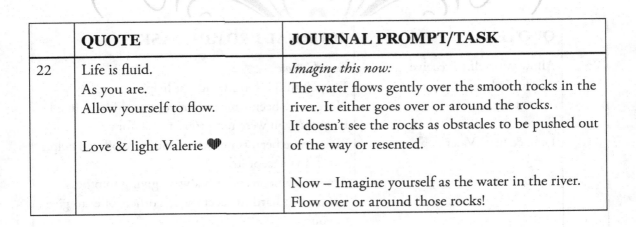	*Imagine this now:* The water flows gently over the smooth rocks in the river. It either goes over or around the rocks. It doesn't see the rocks as obstacles to be pushed out of the way or resented. Now – Imagine yourself as the water in the river. Flow over or around those rocks!

	QUOTE	JOURNAL PROMPT/TASK
23	Allow yourself to receive. Ask for help. Accept it. Love & light Valerie 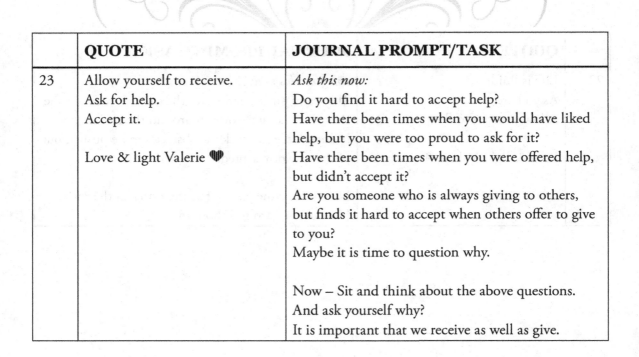	*Ask this now:* Do you find it hard to accept help? Have there been times when you would have liked help, but you were too proud to ask for it? Have there been times when you were offered help, but didn't accept it? Are you someone who is always giving to others, but finds it hard to accept when others offer to give to you? Maybe it is time to question why. Now – Sit and think about the above questions. And ask yourself why? It is important that we receive as well as give.

	QUOTE	JOURNAL PROMPT/TASK
24	In each moment we are making choices. We have free will. Be aware of the choices you are making, because they are creating your life. Love & light Valerie 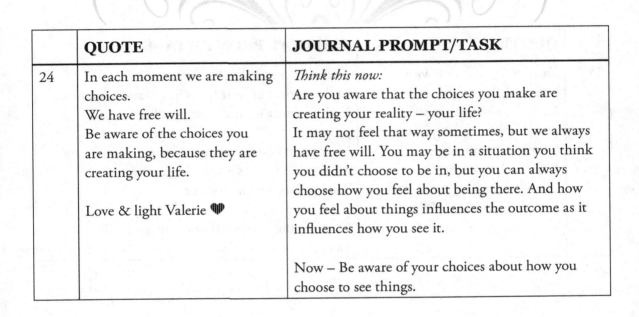	*Think this now:* Are you aware that the choices you make are creating your reality – your life? It may not feel that way sometimes, but we always have free will. You may be in a situation you think you didn't choose to be in, but you can always choose how you feel about being there. And how you feel about things influences the outcome as it influences how you see it. Now – Be aware of your choices about how you choose to see things.

	QUOTE	JOURNAL PROMPT/TASK
25	Each moment is rich with potential. Each moment is rich with possibilities. Savour each moment. Be in each moment. Love & light Valerie 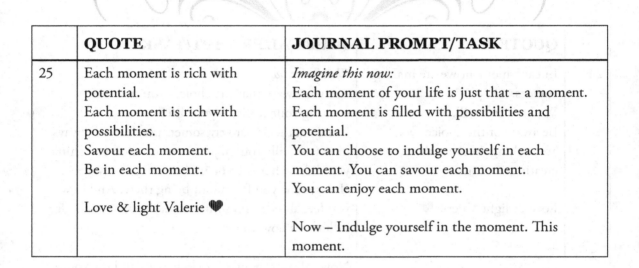	*Imagine this now:* Each moment of your life is just that – a moment. Each moment is filled with possibilities and potential. You can choose to indulge yourself in each moment. You can savour each moment. You can enjoy each moment. Now – Indulge yourself in the moment. This moment.

	QUOTE	JOURNAL PROMPT/TASK
26	Actively direct your thoughts. Quieten your over-thinking. Focus on thoughts of gratitude. Love & light Valerie 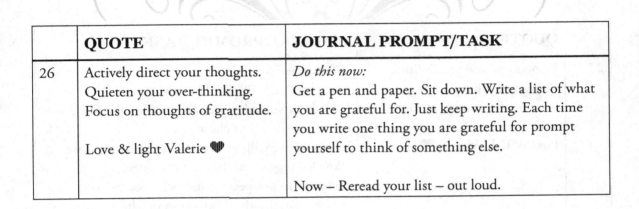	*Do this now:* Get a pen and paper. Sit down. Write a list of what you are grateful for. Just keep writing. Each time you write one thing you are grateful for prompt yourself to think of something else. Now – Reread your list – out loud.

	QUOTE	JOURNAL PROMPT/TASK
27	Be open to new possibilities. Be ready to change. Be ready for transformation. Love & light Valerie 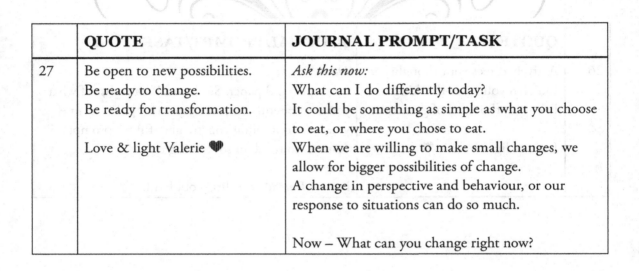	*Ask this now:* What can I do differently today? It could be something as simple as what you choose to eat, or where you chose to eat. When we are willing to make small changes, we allow for bigger possibilities of change. A change in perspective and behaviour, or our response to situations can do so much. Now – What can you change right now?

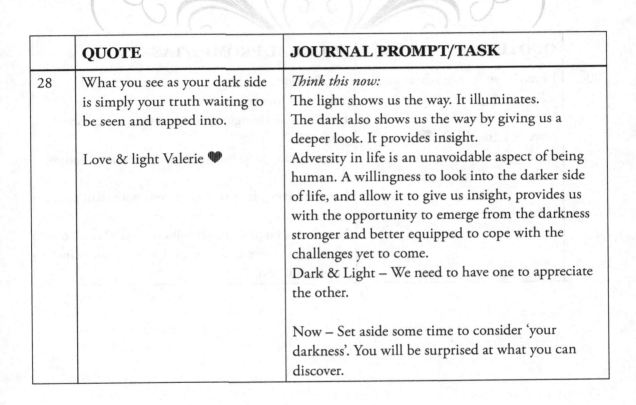

	QUOTE	JOURNAL PROMPT/TASK
28	What you see as your dark side is simply your truth waiting to be seen and tapped into. Love & light Valerie	*Think this now:* The light shows us the way. It illuminates. The dark also shows us the way by giving us a deeper look. It provides insight. Adversity in life is an unavoidable aspect of being human. A willingness to look into the darker side of life, and allow it to give us insight, provides us with the opportunity to emerge from the darkness stronger and better equipped to cope with the challenges yet to come. Dark & Light – We need to have one to appreciate the other. Now – Set aside some time to consider 'your darkness'. You will be surprised at what you can discover.

	QUOTE	JOURNAL PROMPT/TASK
29	Listen to your own advice and follow it. Love & light Valerie ♥	*Do this now:* Take your own advice. Do you have thoughts and ideas that never leave your head? Do you have good intentions that you never follow through on? Do you make plans that are never more than plans? Now – Act on just one thought or idea. Act on one of your good intentions. Act on one of your plans. Just take action!

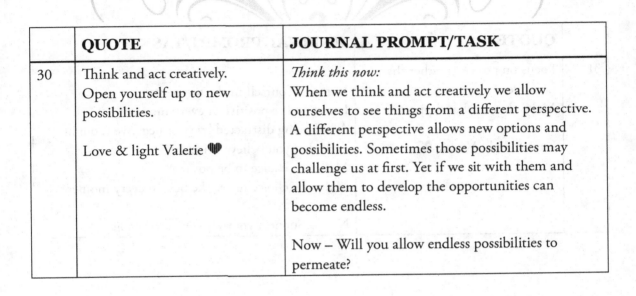

	QUOTE	JOURNAL PROMPT/TASK
30	Think and act creatively. Open yourself up to new possibilities. Love & light Valerie ♥	*Think this now:* When we think and act creatively we allow ourselves to see things from a different perspective. A different perspective allows new options and possibilities. Sometimes those possibilities may challenge us at first. Yet if we sit with them and allow them to develop the opportunities can become endless. Now – Will you allow endless possibilities to permeate?

	QUOTE	JOURNAL PROMPT/TASK
31	Focus on positives rather than negatives. Make choices that support you. Love & light Valerie ♥	*Do this now:* Immerse yourself in the moment. Focus on the positive of every moment. Avoid being distracted by your negative thoughts and what you believe is lacking. Make the choice to be positive. Make the choice to see the best in every moment. Now – Support yourself with your choices.

9. Choose Gratiude Over Regret

	QUOTE	JOURNAL PROMPT/TASK
1	R react E enact G grieve R relive E embarrass T tarnish	*Imagine this now:* We all have times when we have made decisions that weren't in our best interests. And we may think about those times and cringe or shake our heads at ourselves. Yet we can't change what has happened. We cannot undo what was done or not done. Thus, there is little point in regretting those decisions for the rest of our lives. Yes. Think about them and learn from the experience. But, just think for a short time, learn and let go of regret. Now – Are there any regrets you are holding on to? Can you let go?

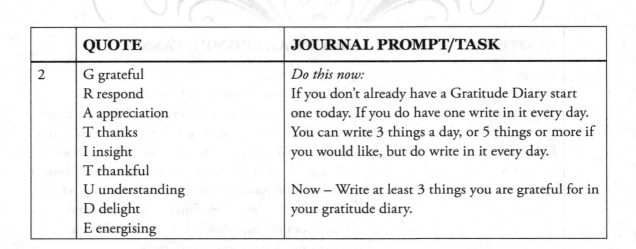

	QUOTE	JOURNAL PROMPT/TASK
2	G grateful R respond A appreciation T thanks I insight T thankful U understanding D delight E energising	*Do this now:* If you don't already have a Gratitude Diary start one today. If you do have one write in it every day. You can write 3 things a day, or 5 things or more if you would like, but do write in it every day. Now – Write at least 3 things you are grateful for in your gratitude diary.

	QUOTE	JOURNAL PROMPT/TASK
3	The more responsible you are the freer you become. Love & light Valerie 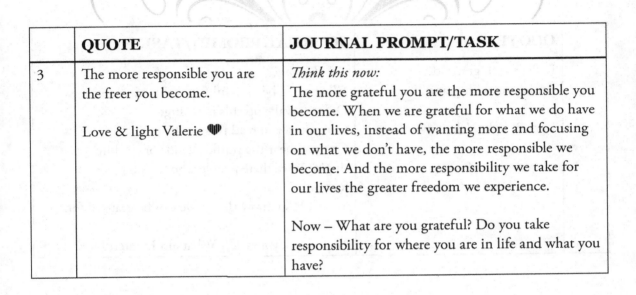	*Think this now:* The more grateful you are the more responsible you become. When we are grateful for what we do have in our lives, instead of wanting more and focusing on what we don't have, the more responsible we become. And the more responsibility we take for our lives the greater freedom we experience. Now – What are you grateful? Do you take responsibility for where you are in life and what you have?

	QUOTE	JOURNAL PROMPT/TASK
4	Reflect with gratitude. Anticipate with gratitude. Love & light Valerie 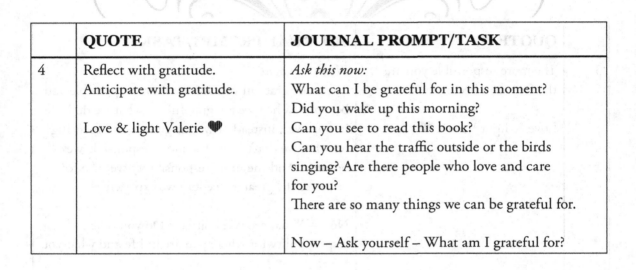	*Ask this now:* What can I be grateful for in this moment? Did you wake up this morning? Can you see to read this book? Can you hear the traffic outside or the birds singing? Are there people who love and care for you? There are so many things we can be grateful for. Now – Ask yourself – What am I grateful for?

	QUOTE	JOURNAL PROMPT/TASK
5	Be the observer of your life and your motivations. Notice and reflect. And be grateful. Love & light Valerie 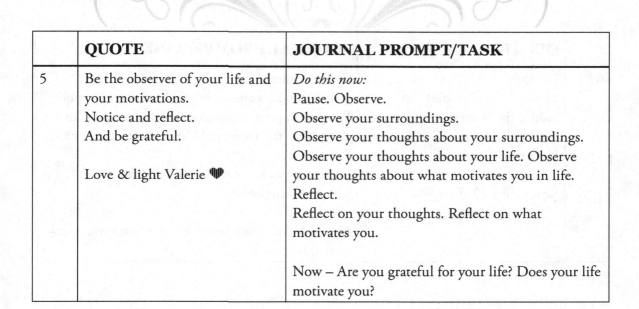	*Do this now:* Pause. Observe. Observe your surroundings. Observe your thoughts about your surroundings. Observe your thoughts about your life. Observe your thoughts about what motivates you in life. Reflect. Reflect on your thoughts. Reflect on what motivates you. Now – Are you grateful for your life? Does your life motivate you?

	QUOTE	JOURNAL PROMPT/TASK
6	Notice! Notice what is around you. Notice the beauty around you. Notice the signs. Notice and appreciate. Love & light Valerie 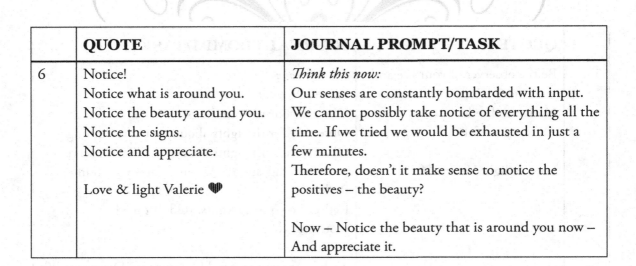	*Think this now:* Our senses are constantly bombarded with input. We cannot possibly take notice of everything all the time. If we tried we would be exhausted in just a few minutes. Therefore, doesn't it make sense to notice the positives – the beauty? Now – Notice the beauty that is around you now – And appreciate it.

	QUOTE	JOURNAL PROMPT/TASK
7	Remember and accept. Even when things don't go exactly as planned, they do go exactly as they are meant to. Love & light Valerie ♥	*Imagine this now:* You have found yourself in a strange situation. Circumstances you have not dealt with before. You feel uncertain of your ability to cope in this situation. Stop and think. How many times before this moment have you been in situations that were unfamiliar and testing of your abilities? Did you cope last time? Or the time before? Or the time before that? I'm guessing if you are reading this – You did! Now – Acknowledge even when you are challenged how capable you are, and that things are always as they are meant to be.

	QUOTE	JOURNAL PROMPT/TASK
8	Appreciate the beauty in your life. Appreciate the not so beautiful in your life. Be grateful. Love & light Valerie 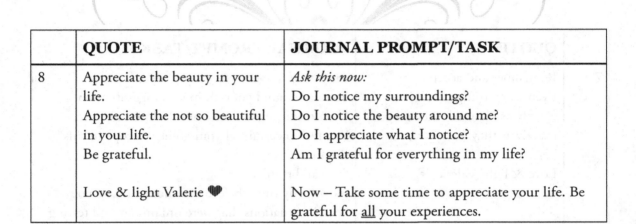	*Ask this now:* Do I notice my surroundings? Do I notice the beauty around me? Do I appreciate what I notice? Am I grateful for everything in my life? Now – Take some time to appreciate your life. Be grateful for <u>all</u> your experiences.

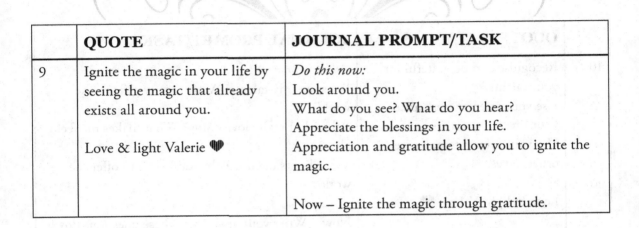

	QUOTE	JOURNAL PROMPT/TASK
9	Ignite the magic in your life by seeing the magic that already exists all around you. Love & light Valerie ♥	*Do this now:* Look around you. What do you see? What do you hear? Appreciate the blessings in your life. Appreciation and gratitude allow you to ignite the magic. Now – Ignite the magic through gratitude.

	QUOTE	JOURNAL PROMPT/TASK
10	Recognise and be grateful for your talents. Use your talents to enhance your life. Use your talents to enhance other's lives. Love & light Valerie 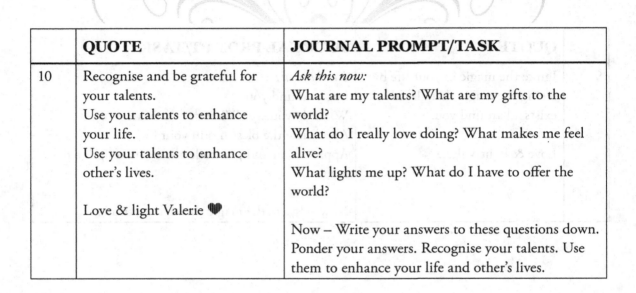	*Ask this now:* What are my talents? What are my gifts to the world? What do I really love doing? What makes me feel alive? What lights me up? What do I have to offer the world? Now – Write your answers to these questions down. Ponder your answers. Recognise your talents. Use them to enhance your life and other's lives.

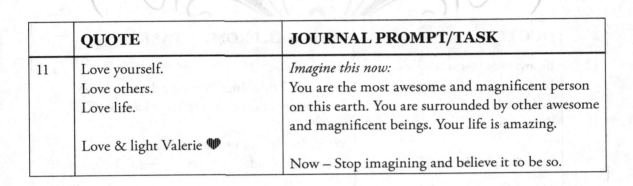

	QUOTE	JOURNAL PROMPT/TASK
11	Love yourself. Love others. Love life. Love & light Valerie ♥	*Imagine this now:* You are the most awesome and magnificent person on this earth. You are surrounded by other awesome and magnificent beings. Your life is amazing. Now – Stop imagining and believe it to be so.

	QUOTE	JOURNAL PROMPT/TASK
12	Be aware of your thoughts. Be aware of your focus. Be humble. Be grateful. Love & light Valerie 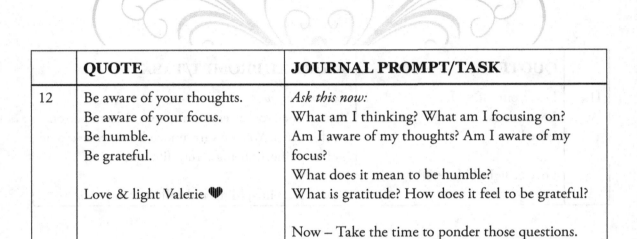	*Ask this now:* What am I thinking? What am I focusing on? Am I aware of my thoughts? Am I aware of my focus? What does it mean to be humble? What is gratitude? How does it feel to be grateful? Now – Take the time to ponder those questions. Record your answers.

	QUOTE	JOURNAL PROMPT/TASK
13	Be aware in each moment. Be present to each moment. Love & light Valerie 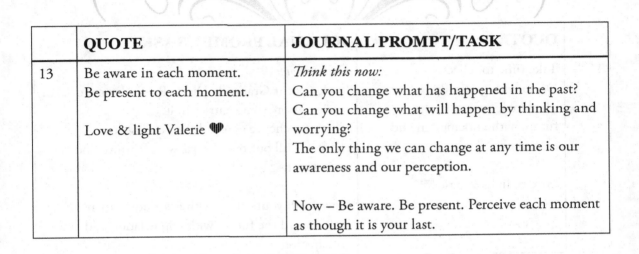	*Think this now:* Can you change what has happened in the past? Can you change what will happen by thinking and worrying? The only thing we can change at any time is our awareness and our perception. Now – Be aware. Be present. Perceive each moment as though it is your last.

	QUOTE	JOURNAL PROMPT/TASK
14	Take time to reflect. Do so with gratitude. Then look toward to the future with anticipation and excitement. Love & light Valerie 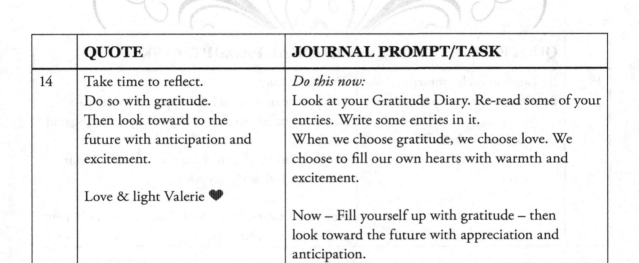	*Do this now:* Look at your Gratitude Diary. Re-read some of your entries. Write some entries in it. When we choose gratitude, we choose love. We choose to fill our own hearts with warmth and excitement. Now – Fill yourself up with gratitude – then look toward the future with appreciation and anticipation.

	QUOTE	JOURNAL PROMPT/TASK
15	The choices you make matter. The steps you take matter. You matter! Love & light Valerie 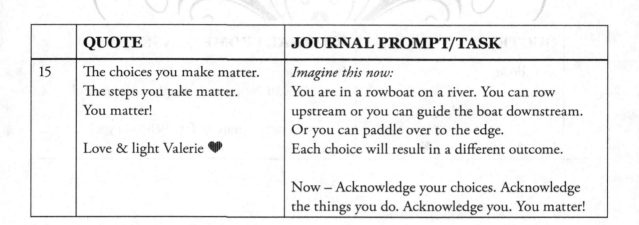	*Imagine this now:* You are in a rowboat on a river. You can row upstream or you can guide the boat downstream. Or you can paddle over to the edge. Each choice will result in a different outcome. Now – Acknowledge your choices. Acknowledge the things you do. Acknowledge you. You matter!

	QUOTE	JOURNAL PROMPT/TASK
16	Slow down. Pause. Take the time to be grateful. Love & light Valerie 🖤	*Do this now:* Pause. Be still. Stop long enough to be grateful. Now – What are grateful for? Who are you grateful for?

	QUOTE	JOURNAL PROMPT/TASK
17	Set your intention for each day. Start each day with gratitude. Stamp each day with your love for you and your love for life. Love & light Valerie 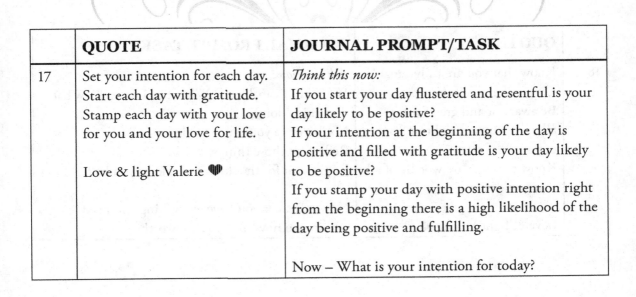	*Think this now:* If you start your day flustered and resentful is your day likely to be positive? If your intention at the beginning of the day is positive and filled with gratitude is your day likely to be positive? If you stamp your day with positive intention right from the beginning there is a high likelihood of the day being positive and fulfilling. Now – What is your intention for today?

	QUOTE	JOURNAL PROMPT/TASK
18	Know that you are fully capable. Let go of any self-doubt. Be aware of and grateful for all that you have right in front of you. Know that you are worthy of all that you desire. Love & light Valerie 🖤	*Ask this now:* What am I capable of? What can I do well? What do I enjoy doing? Maybe write your answers down. Reflect on those things. Be grateful for the skills and talents you have. Now – Realise you have everything you need within you now, and you are worthy.

	QUOTE	JOURNAL PROMPT/TASK
19	Reflect on the past. Envision the future. Be in the present. View all through eyes of love and gratitude. Love & light Valerie 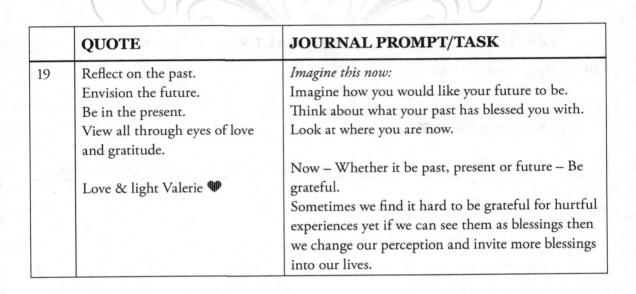	*Imagine this now:* Imagine how you would like your future to be. Think about what your past has blessed you with. Look at where you are now. Now – Whether it be past, present or future – Be grateful. Sometimes we find it hard to be grateful for hurtful experiences yet if we can see them as blessings then we change our perception and invite more blessings into our lives.

	QUOTE	JOURNAL PROMPT/TASK
20	Pause often and look around you with gratitude. Love & light Valerie ❤	*Do this now:* Pause. Look around. Be grateful. Now – What do you see? Can you spot the beauty?

	QUOTE	JOURNAL PROMPT/TASK
21	You get to choose how you respond. It is always your choice. Love & light Valerie ♥	*Think this now:* We can react, or we can respond. It is our choice. Now – What do you choose?

	QUOTE	JOURNAL PROMPT/TASK
22	As you step into appreciation and gratitude you allow yourself to shine. Love & light Valerie 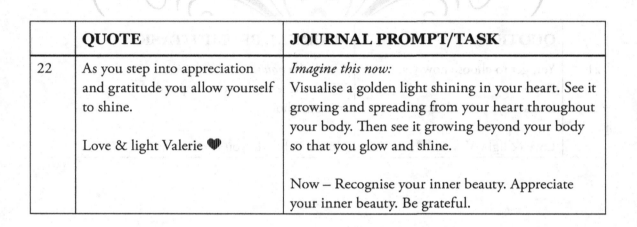	*Imagine this now:* Visualise a golden light shining in your heart. See it growing and spreading from your heart throughout your body. Then see it growing beyond your body so that you glow and shine. Now – Recognise your inner beauty. Appreciate your inner beauty. Be grateful.

	QUOTE	JOURNAL PROMPT/TASK
23	Do something good for yourself. Act in your own best interests. Nurture yourself. Love & light Valerie ♥	*Ask this now:* What can I do that is nurturing for me? What is in my own best interests? Could I go for a walk? Have a bath? Read a book? Make myself a cup of tea? Sit and do nothing? Now – Do something that is good for you.

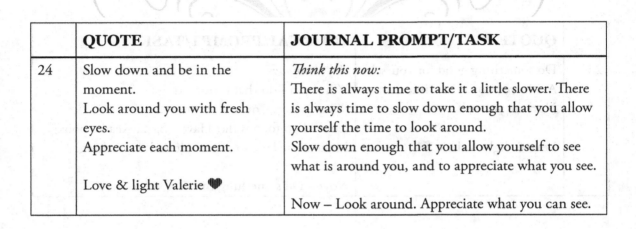

	QUOTE	JOURNAL PROMPT/TASK
24	Slow down and be in the moment. Look around you with fresh eyes. Appreciate each moment. Love & light Valerie 🖤	*Think this now:* There is always time to take it a little slower. There is always time to slow down enough that you allow yourself the time to look around. Slow down enough that you allow yourself to see what is around you, and to appreciate what you see. Now – Look around. Appreciate what you can see.

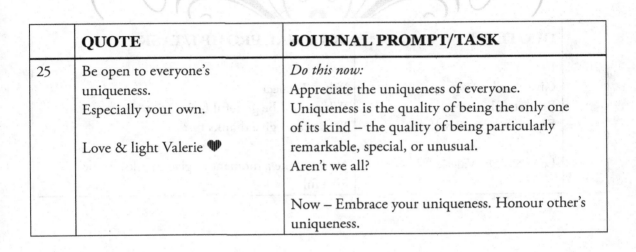

	QUOTE	JOURNAL PROMPT/TASK
25	Be open to everyone's uniqueness. Especially your own. Love & light Valerie 🖤	*Do this now:* Appreciate the uniqueness of everyone. Uniqueness is the quality of being the only one of its kind – the quality of being particularly remarkable, special, or unusual. Aren't we all? Now – Embrace your uniqueness. Honour other's uniqueness.

	QUOTE	JOURNAL PROMPT/TASK
26	Reflect. Give thanks. Be grateful. Especially to yourself. Love & light Valerie ♥	*Ask this now:* When I reflect – What can I be grateful for? What can I give thanks for? Now – Take a moment to give thanks. To be grateful.

	QUOTE	JOURNAL PROMPT/TASK
27	Pause. Reset. Be still. Take time to go within and just be. Love & light Valerie 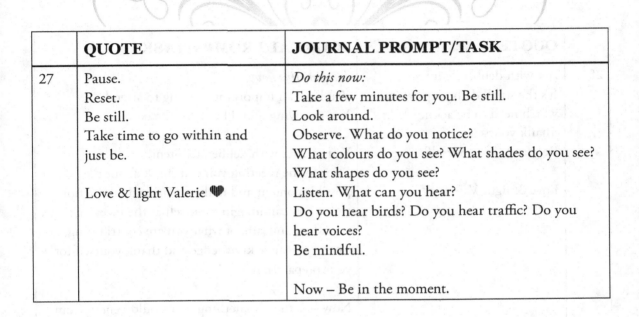	*Do this now:* Take a few minutes for you. Be still. Look around. Observe. What do you notice? What colours do you see? What shades do you see? What shapes do you see? Listen. What can you hear? Do you hear birds? Do you hear traffic? Do you hear voices? Be mindful. Now – Be in the moment.

	QUOTE	JOURNAL PROMPT/TASK
28	Act with deliberate intent. It's the small daily steps we take, which need to be acknowledged. Thank yourself. Be grateful to yourself. Love & light Valerie 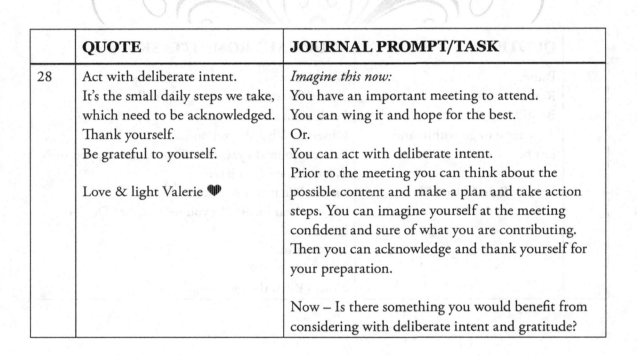	*Imagine this now:* You have an important meeting to attend. You can wing it and hope for the best. Or. You can act with deliberate intent. Prior to the meeting you can think about the possible content and make a plan and take action steps. You can imagine yourself at the meeting confident and sure of what you are contributing. Then you can acknowledge and thank yourself for your preparation. Now – Is there something you would benefit from considering with deliberate intent and gratitude?

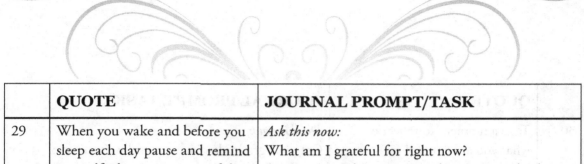

	QUOTE	JOURNAL PROMPT/TASK
29	When you wake and before you sleep each day pause and remind yourself what you are grateful for today. Love & light Valerie ♥	*Ask this now:* What am I grateful for right now? Do I pause each morning and evening to think about what I am grateful for? Now – Make it part of your daily ritual to remind yourself of at least one thing you are grateful for each morning and each evening.

	QUOTE	JOURNAL PROMPT/TASK
30	Take a moment to reflect on what you are grateful for – Your breath. Your sight. Your hearing. Your voice. Your family. Your friends. Your home. And the list goes on ...... Love & light Valerie 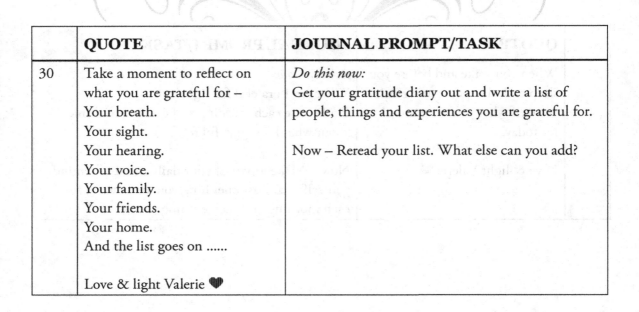	*Do this now:* Get your gratitude diary out and write a list of people, things and experiences you are grateful for. Now – Reread your list. What else can you add?

10. Choose Persistence Over Failure

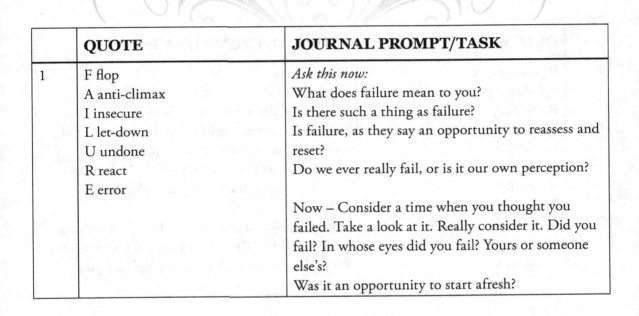

	QUOTE	JOURNAL PROMPT/TASK
1	F flop A anti-climax I insecure L let-down U undone R react E error	*Ask this now:* What does failure mean to you? Is there such a thing as failure? Is failure, as they say an opportunity to reassess and reset? Do we ever really fail, or is it our own perception? Now – Consider a time when you thought you failed. Take a look at it. Really consider it. Did you fail? In whose eyes did you fail? Yours or someone else's? Was it an opportunity to start afresh?

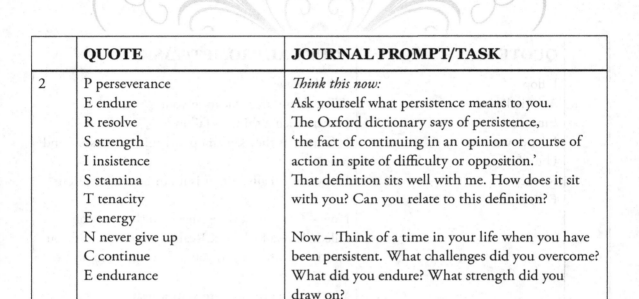

	QUOTE	JOURNAL PROMPT/TASK
2	P perseverance E endure R resolve S strength I insistence S stamina T tenacity E energy N never give up C continue E endurance	*Think this now:* Ask yourself what persistence means to you. The Oxford dictionary says of persistence, 'the fact of continuing in an opinion or course of action in spite of difficulty or opposition.' That definition sits well with me. How does it sit with you? Can you relate to this definition? Now – Think of a time in your life when you have been persistent. What challenges did you overcome? What did you endure? What strength did you draw on?

	QUOTE	JOURNAL PROMPT/TASK
3	Do your work. Push past your self-imposed limitations. Step out of your comfort zone. Love & light Valerie 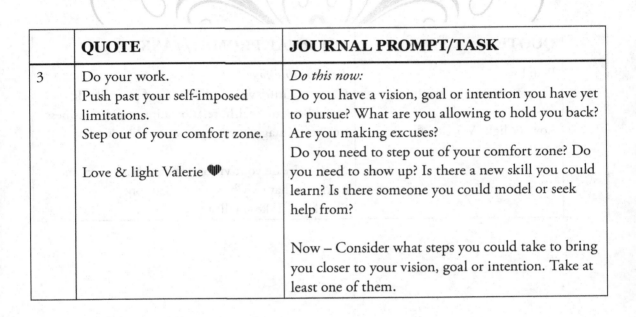	*Do this now:* Do you have a vision, goal or intention you have yet to pursue? What are you allowing to hold you back? Are you making excuses? Do you need to step out of your comfort zone? Do you need to show up? Is there a new skill you could learn? Is there someone you could model or seek help from? Now – Consider what steps you could take to bring you closer to your vision, goal or intention. Take at least one of them.

	QUOTE	JOURNAL PROMPT/TASK
4	Plan big. Try new ways and methods. Love & light Valerie 🖤	*Imagine this now:* Create a future vision of an area of your life. It could be your health, relationships, career, business, finances. Imagine what you would like it to be. Now – Create your vision. Think about ways and methods that may bring it to fruition. Plan big – Take small steps.

	QUOTE	JOURNAL PROMPT/TASK
5	Persistence helps you get something. Consistency helps you keep it. Love & light Valerie 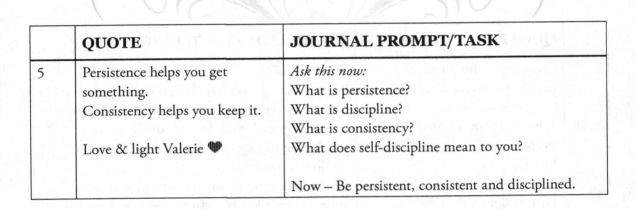	*Ask this now:* What is persistence? What is discipline? What is consistency? What does self-discipline mean to you? Now – Be persistent, consistent and disciplined.

	QUOTE	JOURNAL PROMPT/TASK
6	Every experience in your life has bought you to this moment. Accept and release. With acceptance comes freedom. Be free! Love & light Valerie 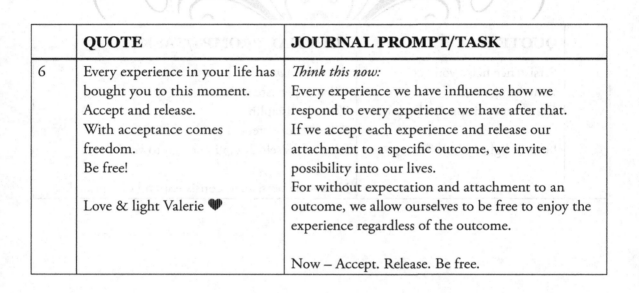	*Think this now:* Every experience we have influences how we respond to every experience we have after that. If we accept each experience and release our attachment to a specific outcome, we invite possibility into our lives. For without expectation and attachment to an outcome, we allow ourselves to be free to enjoy the experience regardless of the outcome. Now – Accept. Release. Be free.

	QUOTE	JOURNAL PROMPT/TASK
7	Think, act and be expansive. Go ahead and share your gifts and talents with the world. Love & light Valerie ♥	*Imagine this now:* You have come to the end of your life and you are reflecting on the life you have lived. You remember things you did as a child. You loved to sing and dance and you did it well, but have you sung or danced lately? You were good with animals and you dreamt of being a vet, but you've spent your working life behind office desks and in board meetings. You loved inventing things that solved problems, but you joined the armed forces. Now – Go back and read the quote again – Then go forth and share your gifts and talents with the world.

	QUOTE	JOURNAL PROMPT/TASK
8	Be aware that your choices each moment install opportunities. Keep your focus steady and true to your goals. Affirm that all your decisions are for your highest good and let them be. Love & light Valerie 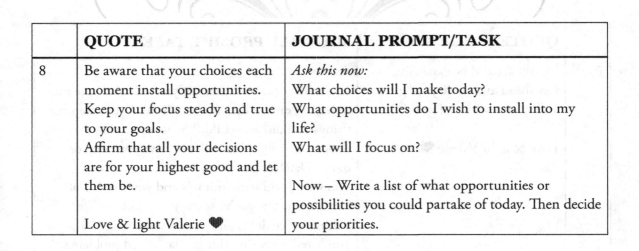	*Ask this now:* What choices will I make today? What opportunities do I wish to install into my life? What will I focus on? Now – Write a list of what opportunities or possibilities you could partake of today. Then decide your priorities.

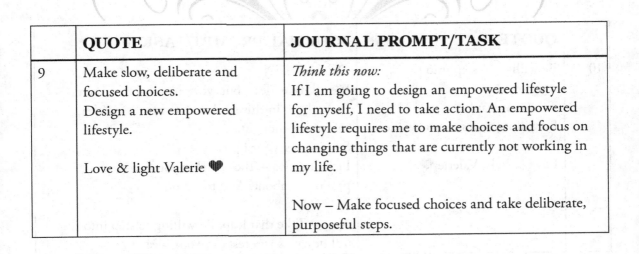

	QUOTE	JOURNAL PROMPT/TASK
9	Make slow, deliberate and focused choices. Design a new empowered lifestyle. Love & light Valerie ♥	*Think this now:* If I am going to design an empowered lifestyle for myself, I need to take action. An empowered lifestyle requires me to make choices and focus on changing things that are currently not working in my life. Now – Make focused choices and take deliberate, purposeful steps.

	QUOTE	JOURNAL PROMPT/TASK
10	Be willing to step into the unknown. Take that leap! Be willing to test out new ideas. Love & light Valerie 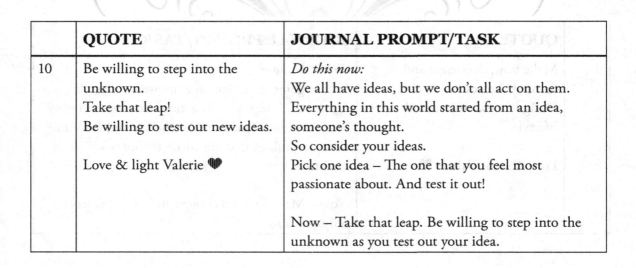	*Do this now:* We all have ideas, but we don't all act on them. Everything in this world started from an idea, someone's thought. So consider your ideas. Pick one idea – The one that you feel most passionate about. And test it out! Now – Take that leap. Be willing to step into the unknown as you test out your idea.

	QUOTE	JOURNAL PROMPT/TASK
11	Consider your actions. Be responsible for your choices. Be responsible for your outcomes. Love & light Valerie 🖤	*Ask this now:* Who is responsible for my choices? Who is responsible for my outcomes? Who is responsible for my actions? Now – If the answer to the above questions isn't 'You' – Ask them again and change your answer.

	QUOTE	JOURNAL PROMPT/TASK
12	The path to success is paved with discipline, persistence and consistency. Love & light Valerie 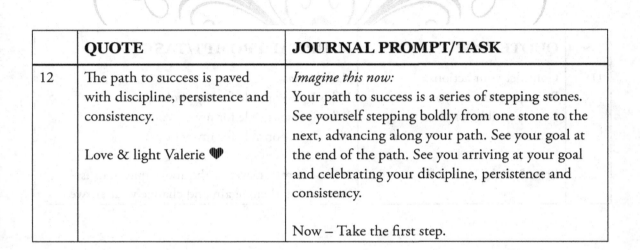	*Imagine this now:* Your path to success is a series of stepping stones. See yourself stepping boldly from one stone to the next, advancing along your path. See your goal at the end of the path. See you arriving at your goal and celebrating your discipline, persistence and consistency. Now – Take the first step.

	QUOTE	JOURNAL PROMPT/TASK
13	Stop and check in. Assess where you are heading. Acknowledge where you have come from. Accept where you are. Love & light Valerie 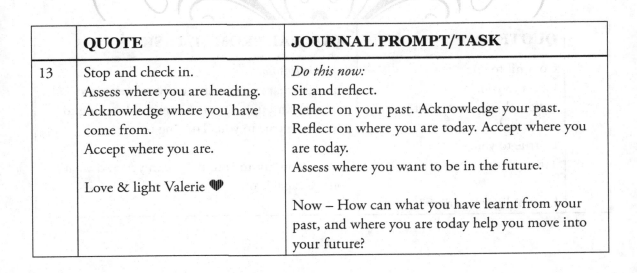	*Do this now:* Sit and reflect. Reflect on your past. Acknowledge your past. Reflect on where you are today. Accept where you are today. Assess where you want to be in the future. Now – How can what you have learnt from your past, and where you are today help you move into your future?

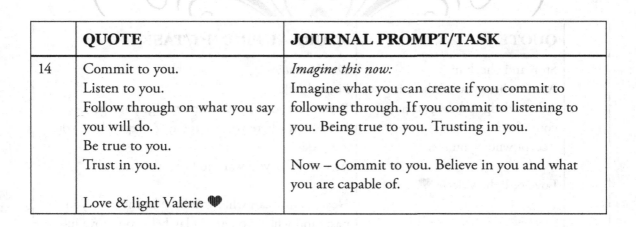

	QUOTE	JOURNAL PROMPT/TASK
14	Commit to you. Listen to you. Follow through on what you say you will do. Be true to you. Trust in you. Love & light Valerie 🖤	*Imagine this now:* Imagine what you can create if you commit to following through. If you commit to listening to you. Being true to you. Trusting in you. Now – Commit to you. Believe in you and what you are capable of.

	QUOTE	JOURNAL PROMPT/TASK
15	Stand tall. Embrace who you are. Allow yourself to shine. Share your unique self with the world. Love & light Valerie ♥	*Think this now:* You are whole and complete. You are all you need. You have everything within you now. Now – Allow yourself to shine. And share your brilliance with the world.

	QUOTE	JOURNAL PROMPT/TASK
16	The world will be ready when you are. One step leads to another. Over time you will realise the big picture of your life. Love & light Valerie 🖤	*Ask this now:* Do you see the big picture of your life? Are you ready to realise it? When you are truly ready to take the steps to create your dream; the world will be ready too. Now – See the big picture. See yourself in the picture. Take a step into that picture.

	QUOTE	JOURNAL PROMPT/TASK
17	Learn and grow from your past. Apply your new wisdom in a way that liberates you. Love & light Valerie 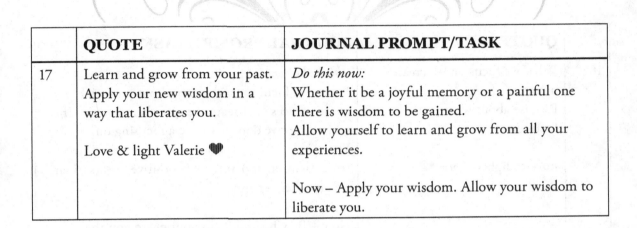	*Do this now:* Whether it be a joyful memory or a painful one there is wisdom to be gained. Allow yourself to learn and grow from all your experiences. Now – Apply your wisdom. Allow your wisdom to liberate you.

	QUOTE	JOURNAL PROMPT/TASK
18	What we focus on we create more of. Be wise about what you focus on. Love & light Valerie 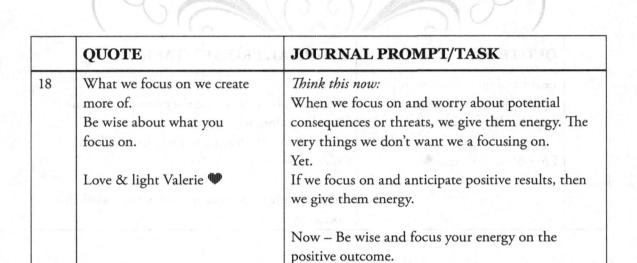	*Think this now:* When we focus on and worry about potential consequences or threats, we give them energy. The very things we don't want we a focusing on. Yet. If we focus on and anticipate positive results, then we give them energy. Now – Be wise and focus your energy on the positive outcome.

	QUOTE	JOURNAL PROMPT/TASK
19	Be still. Be discerning. Be wise. Be gentle with yourself and others. Love & light Valerie 🖤	*Do this now:* Pause and ponder. Connect with your wisdom. Let your wisdom guide you to be discerning. Let your wisdom guide you to be loving and gentle. Now – BE!

	QUOTE	JOURNAL PROMPT/TASK
20	Live with intent. You deserve the best. Make it your intention to give yourself the best. Love & light Valerie 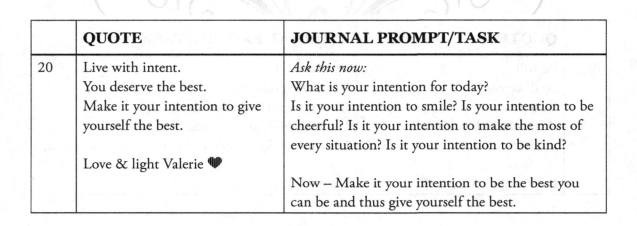	*Ask this now:* What is your intention for today? Is it your intention to smile? Is your intention to be cheerful? Is it your intention to make the most of every situation? Is it your intention to be kind? Now – Make it your intention to be the best you can be and thus give yourself the best.

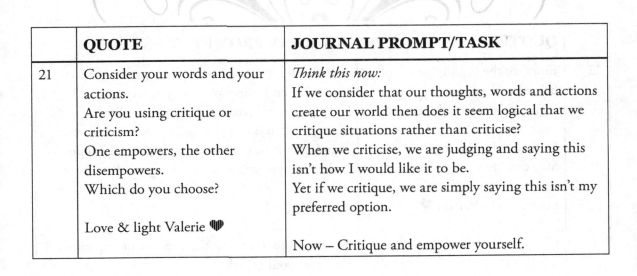

	QUOTE	JOURNAL PROMPT/TASK
21	Consider your words and your actions. Are you using critique or criticism? One empowers, the other disempowers. Which do you choose? Love & light Valerie	*Think this now:* If we consider that our thoughts, words and actions create our world then does it seem logical that we critique situations rather than criticise? When we criticise, we are judging and saying this isn't how I would like it to be. Yet if we critique, we are simply saying this isn't my preferred option. Now – Critique and empower yourself.

	QUOTE	JOURNAL PROMPT/TASK
22	Embrace the healing power of being in the moment. Regularly pause and focus on your breath. Gaze out the window. Step outside. Love & light Valerie 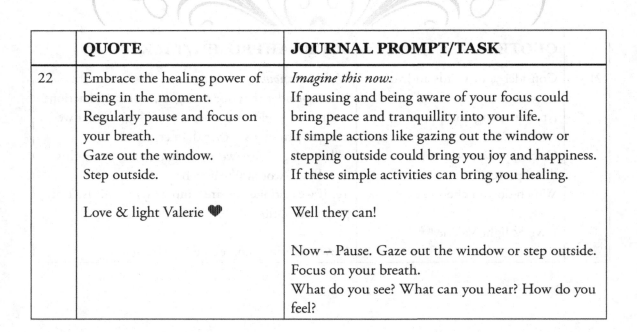	*Imagine this now:* If pausing and being aware of your focus could bring peace and tranquillity into your life. If simple actions like gazing out the window or stepping outside could bring you joy and happiness. If these simple activities can bring you healing. Well they can! Now – Pause. Gaze out the window or step outside. Focus on your breath. What do you see? What can you hear? How do you feel?

	QUOTE	JOURNAL PROMPT/TASK
23	Be still. Stop and listen. Take a moment to see. Be present to the moment and feel. Love & light Valerie ♥	*Do this now:* Look around you. What can you see? What can you see that is green? How many things can you see that are green? Listen. What can you hear? Do you hear birds? Do you hear traffic? How many things can you hear? How do you feel? Now – Take the time to stop and see and listen.

	QUOTE	JOURNAL PROMPT/TASK
24	Be calm and trust. Tell your personality that your soul has it all under control. Follow what you love. Follow your instructions from within. Affirm that you're at one with the Universe and that all comes to you easily. Love & light Valerie 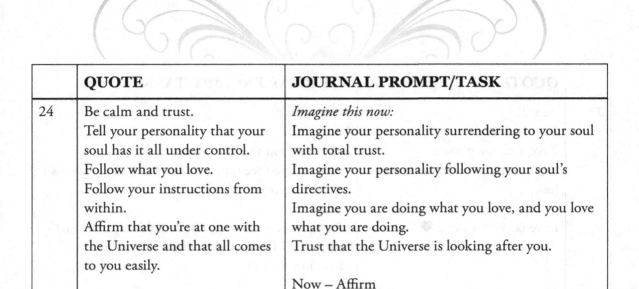	*Imagine this now:* Imagine your personality surrendering to your soul with total trust. Imagine your personality following your soul's directives. Imagine you are doing what you love, and you love what you are doing. Trust that the Universe is looking after you. Now – Affirm 'I am safe.' 'I am always being looked after' 'I trust.'

	QUOTE	JOURNAL PROMPT/TASK
25	Listen. Allow others to speak. Hear them. Love & light Valerie ♥	*Do this now:* Listen to others. Hear what they. Now – Value what others have to say.

	QUOTE	JOURNAL PROMPT/TASK
26	Notice your repetitive thoughts. Do your best not to judge them. Yet do ponder them. Are they moving you forward towards your joy? Or Are they holding you back? Keeping you stuck in your fear? Love & light Valerie 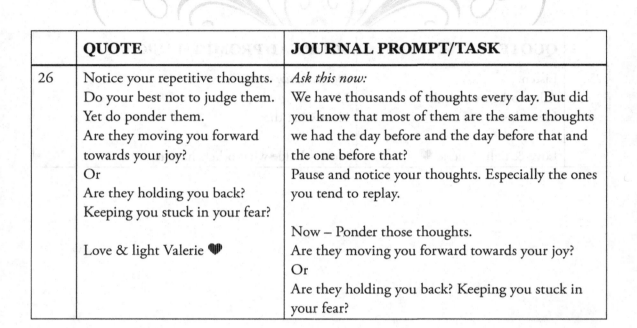	*Ask this now:* We have thousands of thoughts every day. But did you know that most of them are the same thoughts we had the day before and the day before that and the one before that? Pause and notice your thoughts. Especially the ones you tend to replay. Now – Ponder those thoughts. Are they moving you forward towards your joy? Or Are they holding you back? Keeping you stuck in your fear?

	QUOTE	JOURNAL PROMPT/TASK
27	When we take full responsibility for our choices we can learn from our past. We are not trapped by it. There is always more than one path to choose when responding to anyone or anything. It is our choice how we respond to our lives. We are the directors of our life. Love & light Valerie 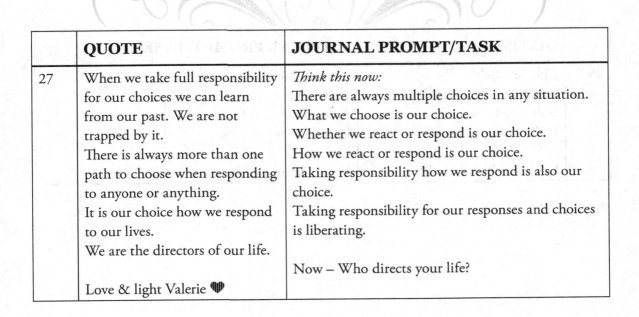	*Think this now:* There are always multiple choices in any situation. What we choose is our choice. Whether we react or respond is our choice. How we react or respond is our choice. Taking responsibility how we respond is also our choice. Taking responsibility for our responses and choices is liberating. Now – Who directs your life?

	QUOTE	JOURNAL PROMPT/TASK
28	Choose wisely. Create your future reality. Build the life you desire. It all begins with you. Love & light Valerie ♥	*Imagine this now:* Do you have a vision of your life? A picture of your future reality? Picture what you desire. Now – Begin building that vision.

	QUOTE	JOURNAL PROMPT/TASK
29	Listen to your inner direction. Make it real. Believe in yourself. Love & light Valerie ♥	*Do this now:* Believing in your inner direction and making it real requires you to believe in yourself. Now – Believe in yourself. Believe in your inner voice.

	QUOTE	JOURNAL PROMPT/TASK
30	Forgive yourself if you have been going into negativity. Seek the positive. Nature continues. Be in a state of gratitude. Love & light Valerie 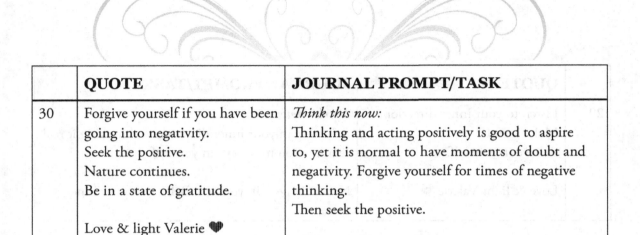	*Think this now:* Thinking and acting positively is good to aspire to, yet it is normal to have moments of doubt and negativity. Forgive yourself for times of negative thinking. Then seek the positive. Now – What do you have to be positive about? What can you be grateful for?

	QUOTE	JOURNAL PROMPT/TASK
31	Act with personal responsibility and you will be right every time. Love & light Valerie 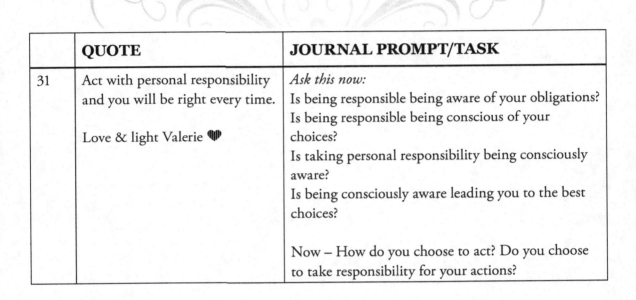	*Ask this now:* Is being responsible being aware of your obligations? Is being responsible being conscious of your choices? Is taking personal responsibility being consciously aware? Is being consciously aware leading you to the best choices? Now – How do you choose to act? Do you choose to take responsibility for your actions?

11. Choose Self-Confidence Over Self-Sabotage

	QUOTE	JOURNAL PROMPT/TASK
1	S subconscious A altering B blocking O obstacle T trouble A assurance G give up E excuses	*Think this now:* If you look up the meaning of sabotage it says to deliberately destroy or damage. To think about that meaning in the context of self-sabotage would encourage most of us to look at our thinking and behaviours. Wouldn't it? Yet how often do we make excuses, give up on our goals, allow setbacks and problems to convince us to stop trying. How often do we sabotage ourselves? Now – Are you aware that forward movement encounters resistance? Do you use resistance as an excuse to give up? To self-sabotage?

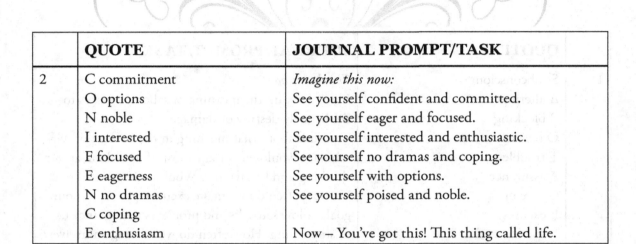

	QUOTE	JOURNAL PROMPT/TASK
2	C commitment O options N noble I interested F focused E eagerness N no dramas C coping E enthusiasm	*Imagine this now:* See yourself confident and committed. See yourself eager and focused. See yourself interested and enthusiastic. See yourself no dramas and coping. See yourself with options. See yourself poised and noble. Now – You've got this! This thing called life.

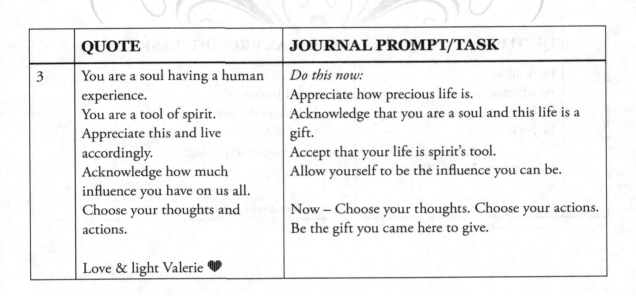

	QUOTE	JOURNAL PROMPT/TASK
3	You are a soul having a human experience. You are a tool of spirit. Appreciate this and live accordingly. Acknowledge how much influence you have on us all. Choose your thoughts and actions. Love & light Valerie	*Do this now:* Appreciate how precious life is. Acknowledge that you are a soul and this life is a gift. Accept that your life is spirit's tool. Allow yourself to be the influence you can be. Now – Choose your thoughts. Choose your actions. Be the gift you came here to give.

	QUOTE	JOURNAL PROMPT/TASK
4	Be flexible. Be adventurous. Be bold and enterprising. Be brave. Love & light Valerie 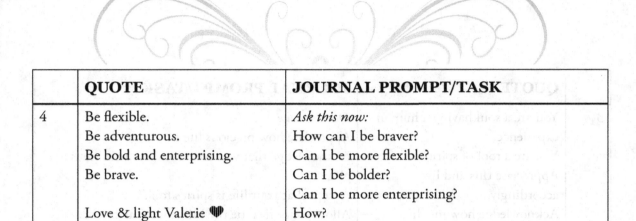	*Ask this now:* How can I be braver? Can I be more flexible? Can I be bolder? Can I be more enterprising? How? Now – Work with your answers.

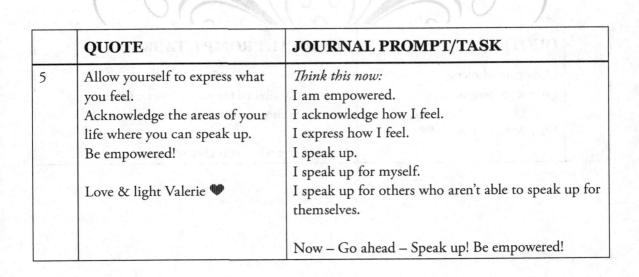

	QUOTE	JOURNAL PROMPT/TASK
5	Allow yourself to express what you feel. Acknowledge the areas of your life where you can speak up. Be empowered! Love & light Valerie 🖤	*Think this now:* I am empowered. I acknowledge how I feel. I express how I feel. I speak up. I speak up for myself. I speak up for others who aren't able to speak up for themselves. Now – Go ahead – Speak up! Be empowered!

	QUOTE	JOURNAL PROMPT/TASK
6	Own your choices. Love what you do. Love & light Valerie 🖤	*Do this now:* Take responsibility for your choices. Own them. Love your choices. Own them. Now – Love what you choose to do.

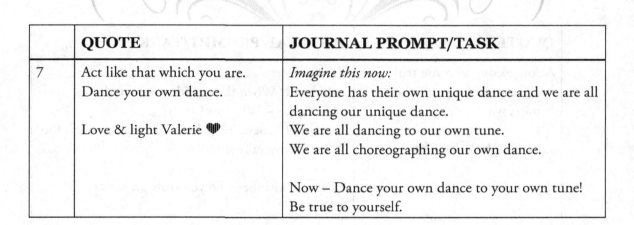

	QUOTE	JOURNAL PROMPT/TASK
7	Act like that which you are. Dance your own dance. Love & light Valerie ♥	*Imagine this now:* Everyone has their own unique dance and we are all dancing our unique dance. We are all dancing to our own tune. We are all choreographing our own dance. Now – Dance your own dance to your own tune! Be true to yourself.

	QUOTE	JOURNAL PROMPT/TASK
8	Acknowledge who you truly are. Make a stand for your truth. It starts with you! Love & light Valerie 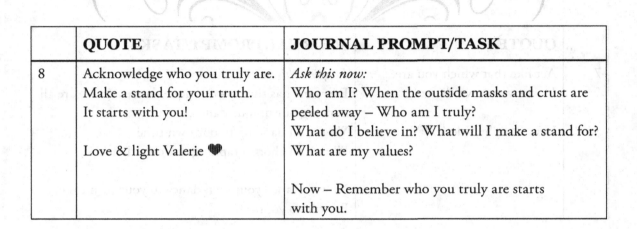	*Ask this now:* Who am I? When the outside masks and crust are peeled away – Who am I truly? What do I believe in? What will I make a stand for? What are my values? Now – Remember who you truly are starts with you.

	QUOTE	JOURNAL PROMPT/TASK
9	Be aware of how capable you are of directing your own destiny. Love & light Valerie ♥	*Think this now:* You are capable. You can choose your vision. You can choose your own direction. You are the director of your life. Now – Recognise your capabilities.

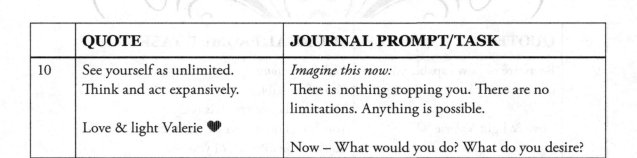

	QUOTE	JOURNAL PROMPT/TASK
10	See yourself as unlimited. Think and act expansively. Love & light Valerie 🖤	*Imagine this now:* There is nothing stopping you. There are no limitations. Anything is possible. Now – What would you do? What do you desire?

	QUOTE	JOURNAL PROMPT/TASK
11	Express yourself without hesitation. Take action with confidence. Love & light Valerie 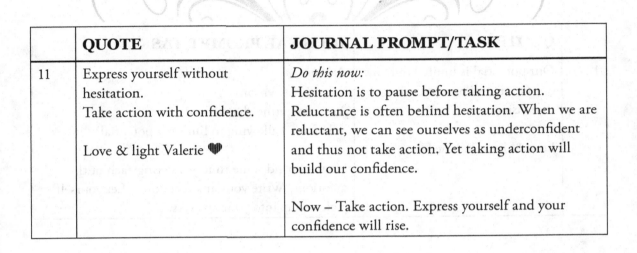	*Do this now:* Hesitation is to pause before taking action. Reluctance is often behind hesitation. When we are reluctant, we can see ourselves as underconfident and thus not take action. Yet taking action will build our confidence. Now – Take action. Express yourself and your confidence will rise.

	QUOTE	JOURNAL PROMPT/TASK
12	Our potential is limited only by our vision and our execution of that vision. Love & light Valerie ♥	*Ask this now:* What is my vision? Am I executing that vision? What am I allowing to limit my potential? Now – Spend some time pondering each of those questions. Write your answers down. Let yourself look deeply into your answers.

	QUOTE	JOURNAL PROMPT/TASK
13	Focus on what you can do here and now. Create an amazing attitude to your life. Love & light Valerie 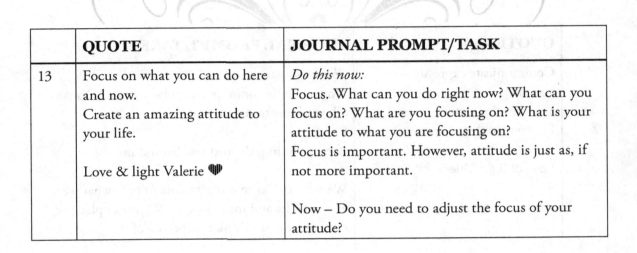	*Do this now:* Focus. What can you do right now? What can you focus on? What are you focusing on? What is your attitude to what you are focusing on? Focus is important. However, attitude is just as, if not more important. Now – Do you need to adjust the focus of your attitude?

	QUOTE	JOURNAL PROMPT/TASK
14	Communicate expressly who you are. You are all you need. Let your soul lead the way. Love & light Valerie 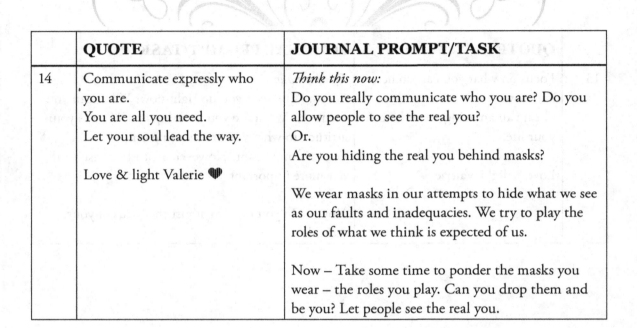	*Think this now:* Do you really communicate who you are? Do you allow people to see the real you? Or. Are you hiding the real you behind masks? We wear masks in our attempts to hide what we see as our faults and inadequacies. We try to play the roles of what we think is expected of us. Now – Take some time to ponder the masks you wear – the roles you play. Can you drop them and be you? Let people see the real you.

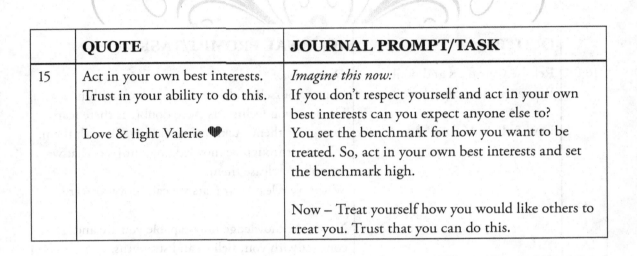

	QUOTE	JOURNAL PROMPT/TASK
15	Act in your own best interests. Trust in your ability to do this. Love & light Valerie 🖤	*Imagine this now:* If you don't respect yourself and act in your own best interests can you expect anyone else to? You set the benchmark for how you want to be treated. So, act in your own best interests and set the benchmark high. Now – Treat yourself how you would like others to treat you. Trust that you can do this.

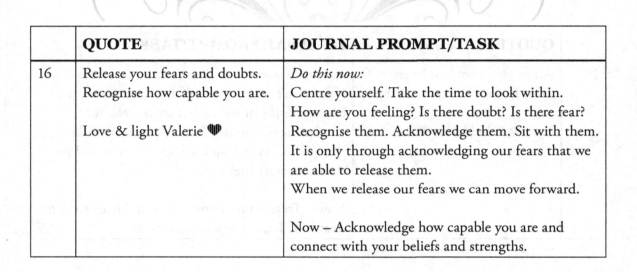

	QUOTE	JOURNAL PROMPT/TASK
16	Release your fears and doubts. Recognise how capable you are. Love & light Valerie ♥	*Do this now:* Centre yourself. Take the time to look within. How are you feeling? Is there doubt? Is there fear? Recognise them. Acknowledge them. Sit with them. It is only through acknowledging our fears that we are able to release them. When we release our fears we can move forward. Now – Acknowledge how capable you are and connect with your beliefs and strengths.

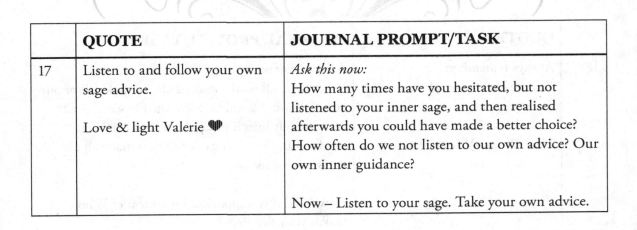

	QUOTE	JOURNAL PROMPT/TASK
17	Listen to and follow your own sage advice. Love & light Valerie 🖤	*Ask this now:* How many times have you hesitated, but not listened to your inner sage, and then realised afterwards you could have made a better choice? How often do we not listen to our own advice? Our own inner guidance? Now – Listen to your sage. Take your own advice.

	QUOTE	JOURNAL PROMPT/TASK
18	Always remember: You are the master of your own destiny. Love & light Valerie ♥	*Imagine this now:* What if we allowed someone else to make all of our choices for us? Would we live the life we desired? Imagine our lives if our parents, our teachers, our friends, our siblings or our pets made all our decisions for us? Now – Who is responsible for your life? Who makes your decisions?

	QUOTE	JOURNAL PROMPT/TASK
19	Are you reliable? Are you trustworthy? Are you committed? – To yourself! – Commit to you. Be reliable. Be the person you trust the most. Love & light Valerie 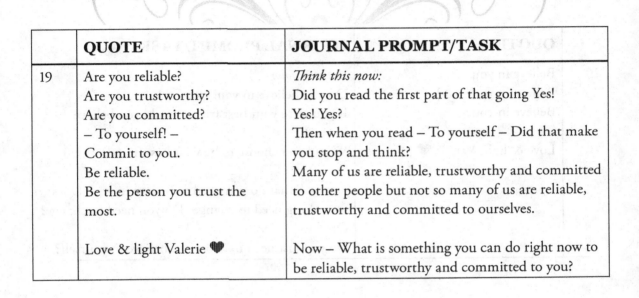	*Think this now:* Did you read the first part of that going Yes! Yes! Yes? Then when you read – To yourself – Did that make you stop and think? Many of us are reliable, trustworthy and committed to other people but not so many of us are reliable, trustworthy and committed to ourselves. Now – What is something you can do right now to be reliable, trustworthy and committed to you?

	QUOTE	JOURNAL PROMPT/TASK
20	Believe in you. Believe in your truth. Believe in you. Love & light Valerie 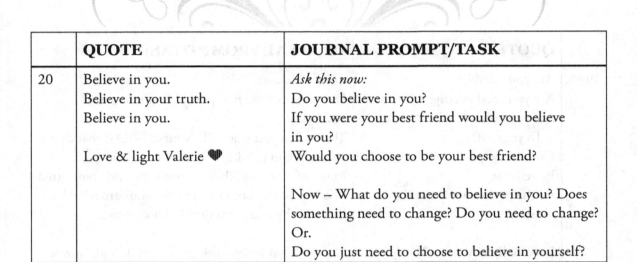	*Ask this now:* Do you believe in you? If you were your best friend would you believe in you? Would you choose to be your best friend? Now – What do you need to believe in you? Does something need to change? Do you need to change? Or. Do you just need to choose to believe in yourself?

	QUOTE	JOURNAL PROMPT/TASK
21	Pause. Put your hands over your heart and say, "I am worthy." Feel it. Love & light Valerie 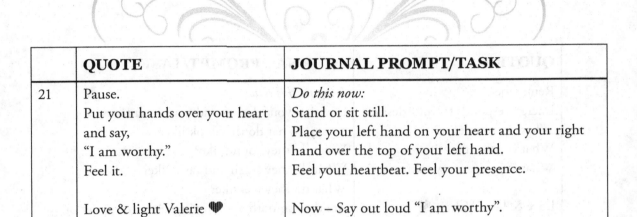	*Do this now:* Stand or sit still. Place your left hand on your heart and your right hand over the top of your left hand. Feel your heartbeat. Feel your presence. Now – Say out loud "I am worthy". Say it like you believe it.

	QUOTE	JOURNAL PROMPT/TASK
22	Remember: Energy responds to your desires. What do you desire? What is your intention? What is your energy asking for? Love & light Valerie 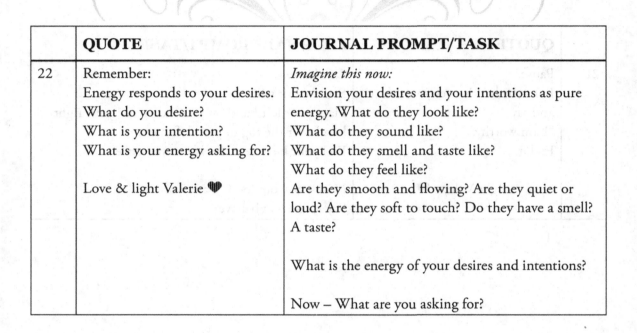	*Imagine this now:* Envision your desires and your intentions as pure energy. What do they look like? What do they sound like? What do they smell and taste like? What do they feel like? Are they smooth and flowing? Are they quiet or loud? Are they soft to touch? Do they have a smell? A taste? What is the energy of your desires and intentions? Now – What are you asking for?

	QUOTE	JOURNAL PROMPT/TASK
23	Be kind, caring and compassionate to yourself. Be gentle with yourself. Find your inner freedom. Love & light Valerie 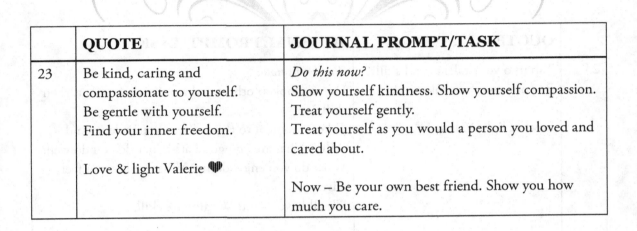	*Do this now?* Show yourself kindness. Show yourself compassion. Treat yourself gently. Treat yourself as you would a person you loved and cared about. Now – Be your own best friend. Show you how much you care.

	QUOTE	JOURNAL PROMPT/TASK
24	Tap into your talents and skills. Be your own best role model. Love & light Valerie ♥	*Think this now:* Do you look at others and admire their talent, their skills? Take a moment to think about your talents and skills. What are you good at? What do you do well? What do you enjoy doing? What makes you feel alive? We all have talent. We all have skills. Now – Tap into your talents and skills. See yourself as your role model.

	QUOTE	JOURNAL PROMPT/TASK
25	You are the Script Writer, Producer, Screenwriter, Editor, Stage Designer and Director of your own movie called 'Life'. Love & light Valerie 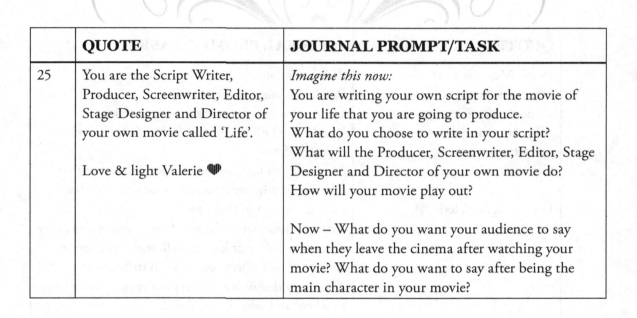	*Imagine this now:* You are writing your own script for the movie of your life that you are going to produce. What do you choose to write in your script? What will the Producer, Screenwriter, Editor, Stage Designer and Director of your own movie do? How will your movie play out? Now – What do you want your audience to say when they leave the cinema after watching your movie? What do you want to say after being the main character in your movie?

	QUOTE	JOURNAL PROMPT/TASK
26	Pause. Muse. Reflect. Honour yourself. Honour your journey. All parts of your journey make you who you are. Celebrate who you are. Love & light Valerie 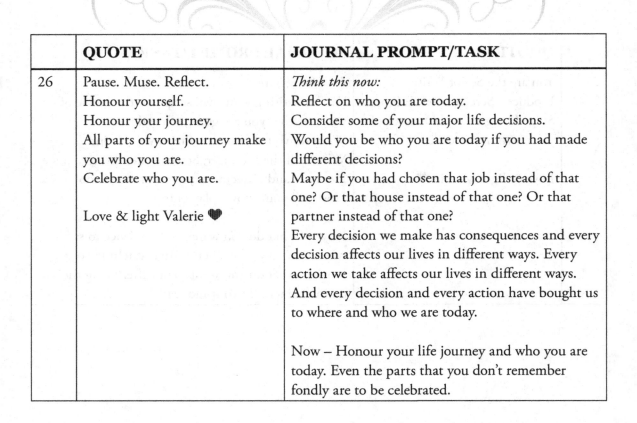	*Think this now:* Reflect on who you are today. Consider some of your major life decisions. Would you be who you are today if you had made different decisions? Maybe if you had chosen that job instead of that one? Or that house instead of that one? Or that partner instead of that one? Every decision we make has consequences and every decision affects our lives in different ways. Every action we take affects our lives in different ways. And every decision and every action have bought us to where and who we are today. Now – Honour your life journey and who you are today. Even the parts that you don't remember fondly are to be celebrated.

	QUOTE	JOURNAL PROMPT/TASK
27	It's time to show yourself. It's time to allow yourself to blossom. Let the world see you. Let the world see your beauty. Let the world see your awesomeness. Love & light Valerie 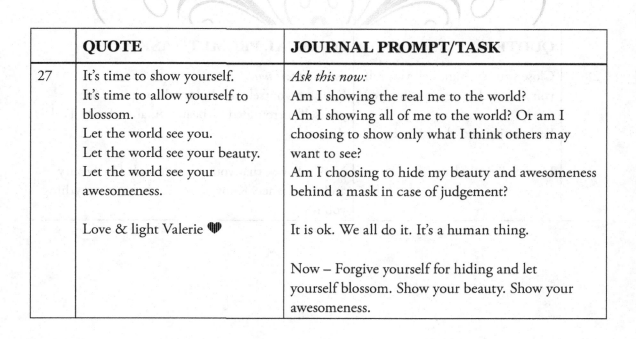	*Ask this now:* Am I showing the real me to the world? Am I showing all of me to the world? Or am I choosing to show only what I think others may want to see? Am I choosing to hide my beauty and awesomeness behind a mask in case of judgement? It is ok. We all do it. It's a human thing. Now – Forgive yourself for hiding and let yourself blossom. Show your beauty. Show your awesomeness.

	QUOTE	JOURNAL PROMPT/TASK
28	Close your eyes and tell yourself you already have everything you need. Feel the joy and abundance. Love & light Valerie 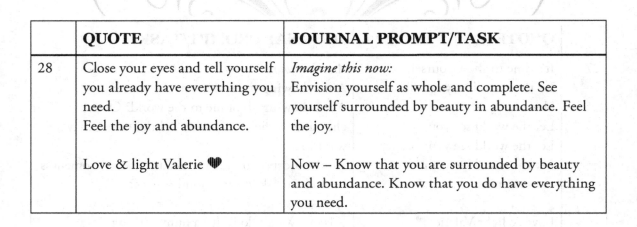	*Imagine this now:* Envision yourself as whole and complete. See yourself surrounded by beauty in abundance. Feel the joy. Now – Know that you are surrounded by beauty and abundance. Know that you do have everything you need.

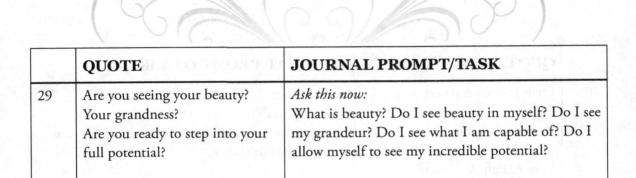

	QUOTE	JOURNAL PROMPT/TASK
29	Are you seeing your beauty? Your grandness? Are you ready to step into your full potential? Love & light Valerie 🖤	*Ask this now:* What is beauty? Do I see beauty in myself? Do I see my grandeur? Do I see what I am capable of? Do I allow myself to see my incredible potential? Now – Step up! Claim your potential.

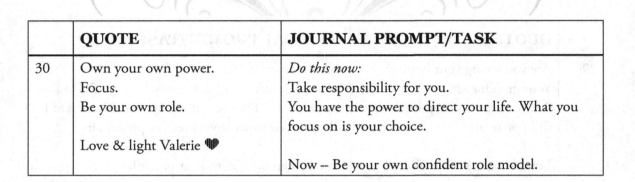

	QUOTE	JOURNAL PROMPT/TASK
30	Own your own power. Focus. Be your own role. Love & light Valerie ♥	*Do this now:* Take responsibility for you. You have the power to direct your life. What you focus on is your choice. Now -- Be your own confident role model.

12. Choose Celebration Over Criticism

	QUOTE	JOURNAL PROMPT/TASK
1	C censure R reproach I irritation T touchy I inconsiderate C condemnation I irrational S stern M mistake oriented	*Think this now:* How often have you criticised yourself or others? We all have a tendency to criticise. However, does it make a difference? Does it result in improvement? Critical appraisal or constructive feedback are far more worthwhile than criticism. Criticism just tells us what we are doing badly in the eyes of the one criticising (often ourselves), yet it doesn't give us anything upon which to improve our performance. Now – Constructive feedback! How would you approach someone who had just made a mistake?

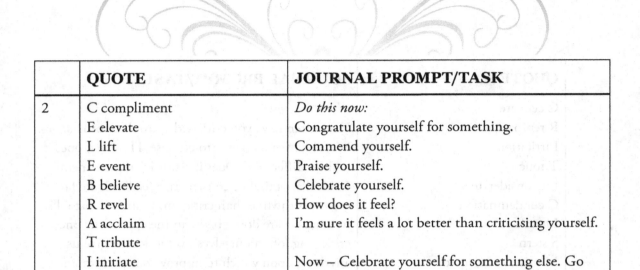

	QUOTE	JOURNAL PROMPT/TASK
2	C compliment E elevate L lift E event B believe R revel A acclaim T tribute I initiate O honour N nice	*Do this now:* Congratulate yourself for something. Commend yourself. Praise yourself. Celebrate yourself. How does it feel? I'm sure it feels a lot better than criticising yourself. Now – Celebrate yourself for something else. Go on – Praise yourself. Commend yourself. Honour yourself. Acclaim how good you are. Pay tribute to you!

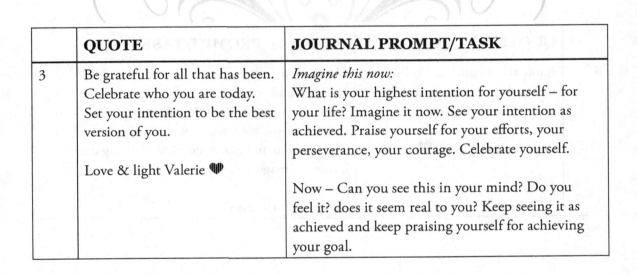

	QUOTE	JOURNAL PROMPT/TASK
3	Be grateful for all that has been. Celebrate who you are today. Set your intention to be the best version of you. Love & light Valerie	*Imagine this now:* What is your highest intention for yourself – for your life? Imagine it now. See your intention as achieved. Praise yourself for your efforts, your perseverance, your courage. Celebrate yourself. Now – Can you see this in your mind? Do you feel it? does it seem real to you? Keep seeing it as achieved and keep praising yourself for achieving your goal.

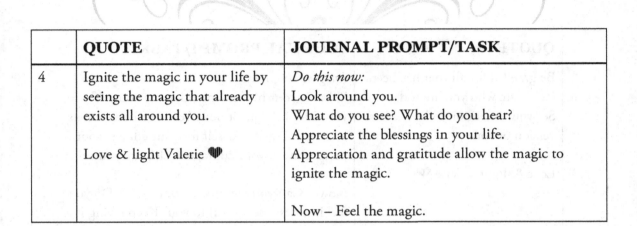

	QUOTE	JOURNAL PROMPT/TASK
4	Ignite the magic in your life by seeing the magic that already exists all around you. Love & light Valerie ♥	*Do this now:* Look around you. What do you see? What do you hear? Appreciate the blessings in your life. Appreciation and gratitude allow the magic to ignite the magic. Now – Feel the magic.

	QUOTE	JOURNAL PROMPT/TASK
5	Take a practical approach to your future. Be discerning and thorough in your choices. Take strong, solid steps. Love & light Valerie 🖤	*Ask this now:* What do you focus your attention on? Your successes? Or. Your mistakes and what you consider your failures? It is your choice who and what you give your precious energy too and where you focus your attention and your intention. Now – Focus on your successes – Praise and celebrate them.

	QUOTE	JOURNAL PROMPT/TASK
6	Believe in yourself. Believe in your individuality. Believe in you! Love & light Valerie 🖤	*Do this now:* According to dictionary.com – 'Only if one believes in something can one act purposefully.' So let's start with self-belief. Now – Believe in you! Believe in what you are capable of and what you can achieve.

	QUOTE	JOURNAL PROMPT/TASK
7	Pause. Put your hands on your heart. Connect with your soul. Feel the love. Love & light Valerie 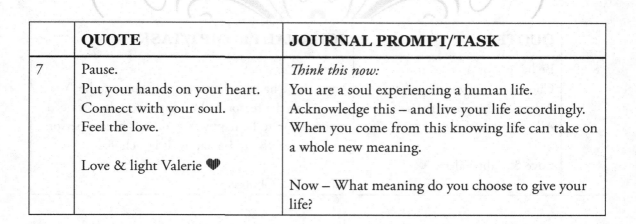	*Think this now:* You are a soul experiencing a human life. Acknowledge this – and live your life accordingly. When you come from this knowing life can take on a whole new meaning. Now – What meaning do you choose to give your life?

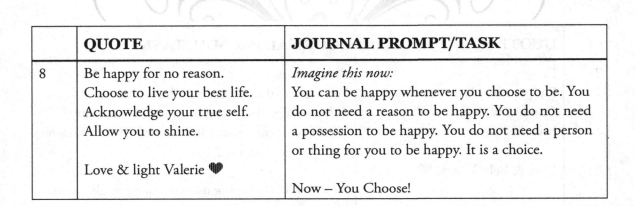

	QUOTE	JOURNAL PROMPT/TASK
8	Be happy for no reason. Choose to live your best life. Acknowledge your true self. Allow you to shine. Love & light Valerie ♥	*Imagine this now:* You can be happy whenever you choose to be. You do not need a reason to be happy. You do not need a possession to be happy. You do not need a person or thing for you to be happy. It is a choice. Now -- You Choose!

	QUOTE	JOURNAL PROMPT/TASK
9	When you action your desires answers start coming. When you support yourself you feel supported. When you value yourself you feel worthy. Love & light Valerie 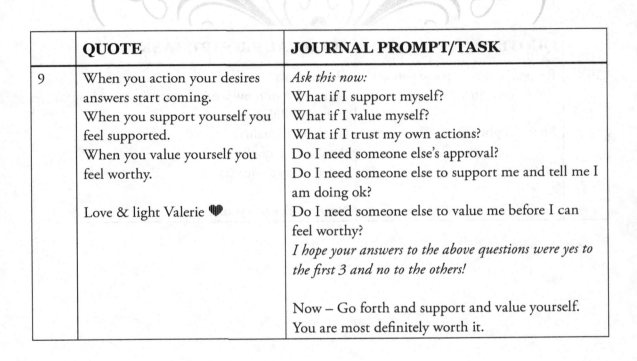	*Ask this now:* What if I support myself? What if I value myself? What if I trust my own actions? Do I need someone else's approval? Do I need someone else to support me and tell me I am doing ok? Do I need someone else to value me before I can feel worthy? *I hope your answers to the above questions were yes to the first 3 and no to the others!* Now – Go forth and support and value yourself. You are most definitely worth it.

	QUOTE	JOURNAL PROMPT/TASK
10	Recognise how capable you are. Celebrate yourself. Love & light Valerie	*Do this now:* Make a list or draw a mind map of your strengths and capabilities. Circle each quality. Ponder each quality. Celebrate each quality. Now – Celebrate you!

	QUOTE	JOURNAL PROMPT/TASK
11	Be in awe of yourself and your journey through life. Love & light Valerie 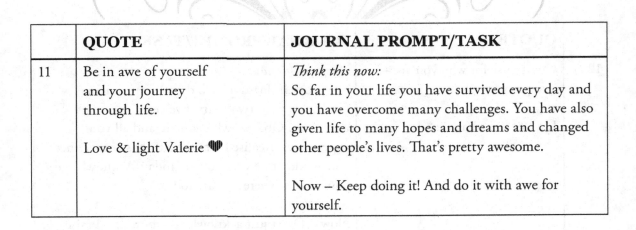	*Think this now:* So far in your life you have survived every day and you have overcome many challenges. You have also given life to many hopes and dreams and changed other people's lives. That's pretty awesome. Now – Keep doing it! And do it with awe for yourself.

	QUOTE	JOURNAL PROMPT/TASK
12	Give praise for who you are – You got yourself here. Love & light Valerie 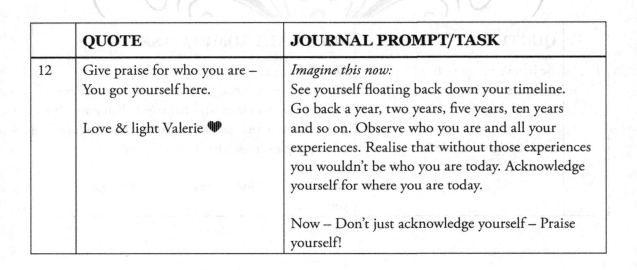	*Imagine this now:* See yourself floating back down your timeline. Go back a year, two years, five years, ten years and so on. Observe who you are and all your experiences. Realise that without those experiences you wouldn't be who you are today. Acknowledge yourself for where you are today. Now – Don't just acknowledge yourself – Praise yourself!

	QUOTE	JOURNAL PROMPT/TASK
13	Stop! Remind yourself how capable and resilient you truly are. Take ownership of your true value and worth. You are priceless! Love & light Valerie 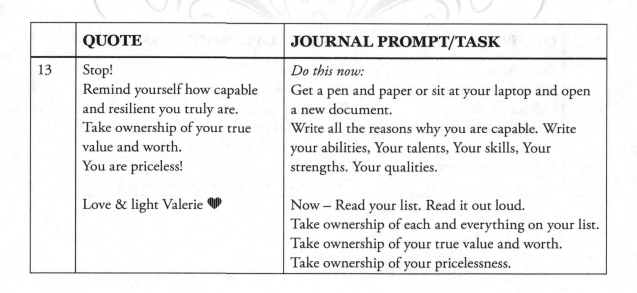	*Do this now:* Get a pen and paper or sit at your laptop and open a new document. Write all the reasons why you are capable. Write your abilities, Your talents, Your skills, Your strengths. Your qualities. Now – Read your list. Read it out loud. Take ownership of each and everything on your list. Take ownership of your true value and worth. Take ownership of your pricelessness.

	QUOTE	JOURNAL PROMPT/TASK
14	Pause often and be in awe of yourself. Celebrate you. You are worthy. Love & light Valerie 🖤	*Ask this now:* What do I enjoy doing? What am I good at? What do I do well? What can I celebrate about me? Now – Celebrate you! Be in awe of you!

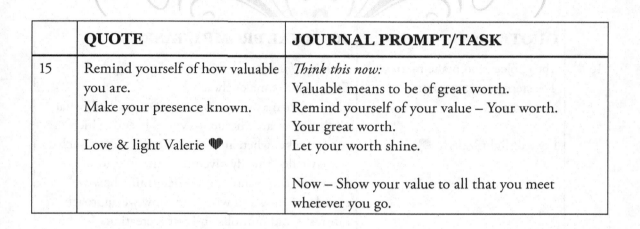

	QUOTE	JOURNAL PROMPT/TASK
15	Remind yourself of how valuable you are. Make your presence known. Love & light Valerie 🖤	*Think this now:* Valuable means to be of great worth. Remind yourself of your value – Your worth. Your great worth. Let your worth shine. Now – Show your value to all that you meet wherever you go.

	QUOTE	JOURNAL PROMPT/TASK
16	The choices you make matter. The steps you take matter. You matter! Love & light Valerie ♥	*Imagine this now:* Every day we make choices. Choices such as what time to get out of bed, what clothes to wear, whether to visit a friend, which road to take, when and what to eat. Choices such as these we don't really give much thought to. However, those choices also determine how we spend our time and who with, how we approach our tasks and our jobs and our recreation. Even the small choices matter. Now – Consider your choices. It is your choice what you choose to think about and how you choose to approach things.

	QUOTE	JOURNAL PROMPT/TASK
17	Be aware of your focus. Focus on what uplifts you. Love & light Valerie 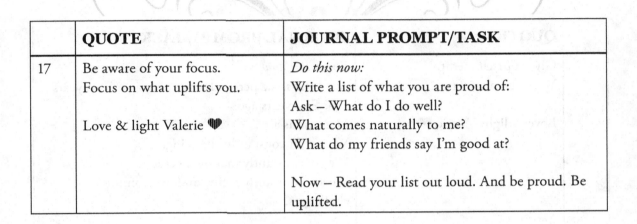	*Do this now:* Write a list of what you are proud of: Ask – What do I do well? What comes naturally to me? What do my friends say I'm good at? Now – Read your list out loud. And be proud. Be uplifted.

	QUOTE	JOURNAL PROMPT/TASK
18	Give yourself credit. You've come so far. Love & light Valerie 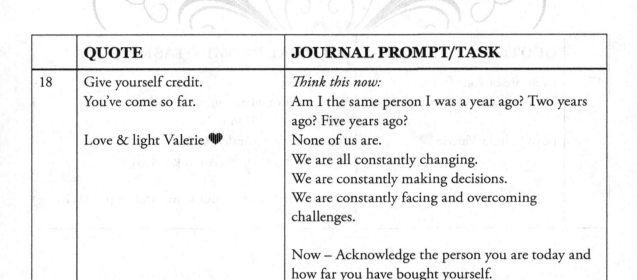	*Think this now:* Am I the same person I was a year ago? Two years ago? Five years ago? None of us are. We are all constantly changing. We are constantly making decisions. We are constantly facing and overcoming challenges. Now – Acknowledge the person you are today and how far you have bought yourself.

	QUOTE	JOURNAL PROMPT/TASK
19	Give yourself permission and have the courage to be you. Love & light Valerie ♥	*Ask this now:* Do you need someone else's permission to be you? If you think you do, who's permission? Now – Have courage and be you. Remember you are unique.

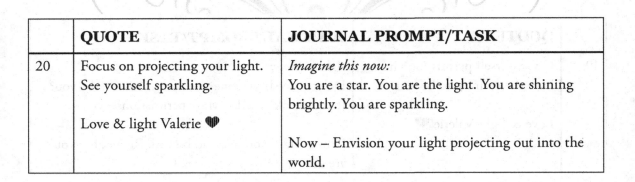

	QUOTE	JOURNAL PROMPT/TASK
20	Focus on projecting your light. See yourself sparkling. Love & light Valerie ♥	*Imagine this now:* You are a star. You are the light. You are shining brightly. You are sparkling. Now – Envision your light projecting out into the world.

	QUOTE	JOURNAL PROMPT/TASK
21	Take the time to be still and connect with your soul. What is it that you wish to share with the world? You make a difference! Remember this always. Love & light Valerie ♥	*Do this now:* Find a quiet spot – In nature would be ideal. Sit comfortably – I suggest you have a notebook and something to write with. Take a moment to focus into your heart. – You might like to place your hands over your heart to aid your focus. Now – Ask – What do I have to share with others? What do I have that will make a difference to others? Write down whatever comes to you. Work with that.

	QUOTE	JOURNAL PROMPT/TASK
22	Follow the call of your soul. Be willing to try a new way of being. Allow yourself to shine. Love & light Valerie ❤	*Ask this now:* What is my soul saying to me? Am I listening? Am I willing to try something different? Am I willing to be different today than I was yesterday? Am I willing to show my talents to the world? Now – Let yourself shine. Let the world see you.

	QUOTE	JOURNAL PROMPT/TASK
23	When you speak – Speak words that inspire and uplift. Rather than criticise and denigrate. Especially to yourself. Love & light Valerie 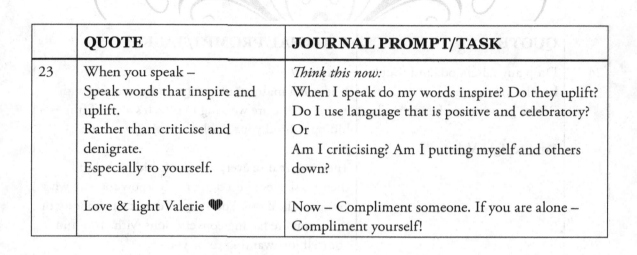	*Think this now:* When I speak do my words inspire? Do they uplift? Do I use language that is positive and celebratory? Or Am I criticising? Am I putting myself and others down? Now – Compliment someone. If you are alone – Compliment yourself!

	QUOTE	JOURNAL PROMPT/TASK
24	Drop any falsehood, and simply be who you are. Be the genuine, authentic you! Love & light Valerie ♥	*Imagine this now:* You're at a masquerade party, and you along with everyone else are wearing masks. It's a bit of fun hiding behind your mask and being someone you're not. Then you realise everyone else is hiding behind their masks too. You don't really know for sure who you are talking to. You start to doubt the honesty of those you are having conversations with. You find yourself just wanting to be you. Can you relate this scene to your life? How often do we choose to wear a mask and hide behind an identity? Do we wear masks to hide what we think others will criticise or judge? Now – Consider the masks that you wear. What are you trying to hide? What are you afraid of people seeing? Would it be ok for them to see the real you? The genuine you?

	QUOTE	JOURNAL PROMPT/TASK
25	Recognise the beauty and magnificence within you. Love & light Valerie 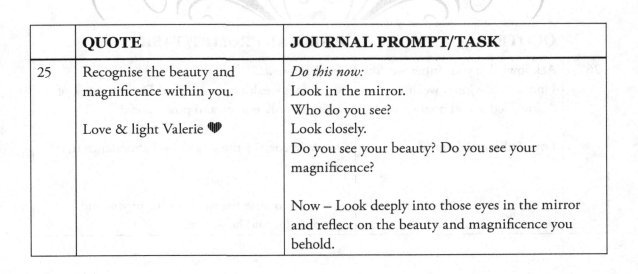	*Do this now:* Look in the mirror. Who do you see? Look closely. Do you see your beauty? Do you see your magnificence? Now – Look deeply into those eyes in the mirror and reflect on the beauty and magnificence you behold.

	QUOTE	JOURNAL PROMPT/TASK
26	Acknowledge your inner wealth. Honour your inner wealth. Acknowledge and honour you! Love & light Valerie ♥	*Think this now:* What does wealth mean to you? Do you think of wealth as only money and possessions? Or Do you recognise the wealth and abundance that is within you? Now – Recognise the wealth with in you and acknowledge and honour it.

Valerie Rhee Driver

	QUOTE	JOURNAL PROMPT/TASK
27	Be aware of any negative self-talk. Catch yourself in the act. Choose your thoughts and your words to empower your life. Love & light Valerie 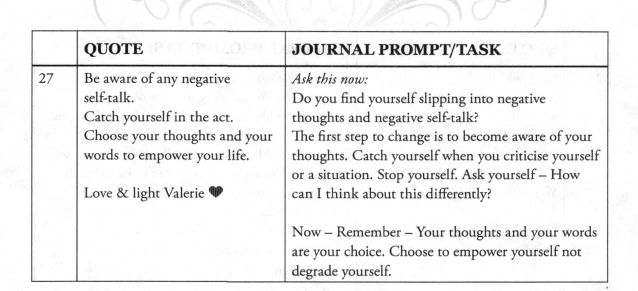	*Ask this now:* Do you find yourself slipping into negative thoughts and negative self-talk? The first step to change is to become aware of your thoughts. Catch yourself when you criticise yourself or a situation. Stop yourself. Ask yourself – How can I think about this differently? Now – Remember – Your thoughts and your words are your choice. Choose to empower yourself not degrade yourself.

	QUOTE	JOURNAL PROMPT/TASK
28	Look within. Acknowledge all aspects of yourself. Accept all of you. Love all of you. You are enough. You are loveable. Love & light Valerie 🖤	*Imagine this now:* Imagine you are standing in front of yourself. Take a good look at yourself. Stare deeply into your eyes. See yourself. All of yourself. All aspects of yourself. Those you like and those you don't like so much. Accept all of you. Love all of you. Now – Say these words. I am enough. I am loveable.

	QUOTE	JOURNAL PROMPT/TASK
29	Honour who you are. All of you. Love who you are. All of you. Love & light Valerie 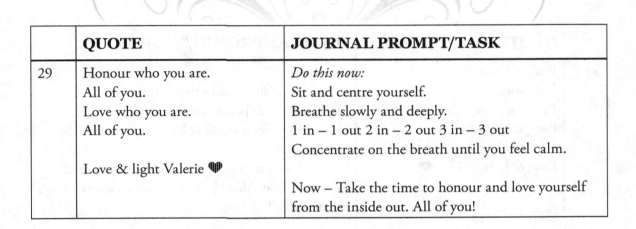	*Do this now:* Sit and centre yourself. Breathe slowly and deeply. 1 in – 1 out 2 in – 2 out 3 in – 3 out Concentrate on the breath until you feel calm. Now – Take the time to honour and love yourself from the inside out. All of you!

	QUOTE	JOURNAL PROMPT/TASK
30	Embrace you. Love you. Be the love you wish to see in the (your) world. Love & light Valerie 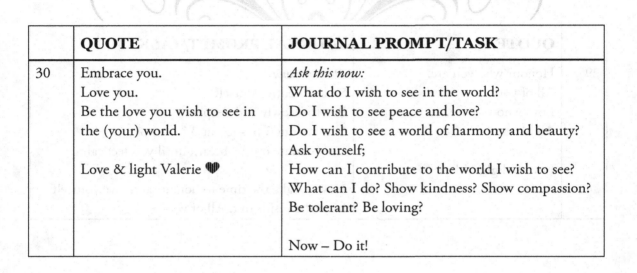	*Ask this now:* What do I wish to see in the world? Do I wish to see peace and love? Do I wish to see a world of harmony and beauty? Ask yourself; How can I contribute to the world I wish to see? What can I do? Show kindness? Show compassion? Be tolerant? Be loving? Now – Do it!

	QUOTE	JOURNAL PROMPT/TASK
31	Be true to yourself. Be your true self. Love & light Valerie 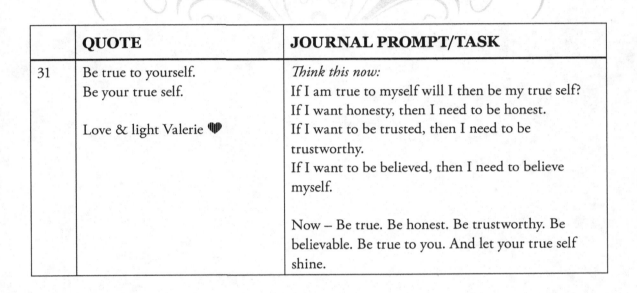	*Think this now:* If I am true to myself will I then be my true self? If I want honesty, then I need to be honest. If I want to be trusted, then I need to be trustworthy. If I want to be believed, then I need to believe myself. Now – Be true. Be honest. Be trustworthy. Be believable. Be true to you. And let your true self shine.

I have totally enjoyed and felt inspired writing this book and sharing so many of my quotes with you. I hope, as it was my intention in writing this book that you, the reader, will enjoy reading the quotes and completing the tasks and be inspired: Inspired to choose Courage over Fear, Action over Perfection, Trust over Doubt, Clarity over Confusion, Joy over Sadness, Hope over Despair, Focus over Distraction, Less over More (Simplicity over Complication), Gratitude over Regret, Persistence over Failure, Self-confidence over Self-sabotage, and Celebration over Criticism.

Thank you for reading 'My Inspirations for You'.

Love Rhee

One last quote for this book: (It will not be the last quote though).

Close your eyes and be still.
Breathe deeply in and out.
Feel your presence.
Feel your love.
Remember – You are love. ♥

Love & light Valerie ♥